The Candidates 1980

The Candidates 1980: Where They Stand

American Enterprise Institute for Public Policy Research
Washington, D.C.

This book is part of ongoing AEI research partially funded by a grant from the LTV Corporation.

Library of Congress Catalog Card No. 80-666

ISBN 0-8447-1336-8

Printed in the United States of America

Preface

The Candidates 1980: Where They Stand represents a major effort by the American Enterprise Institute for Public Policy Research to contribute to educated and informed public discourse on the issues facing the American people not only in the 1980 presidential campaign but throughout the 1980s. The book is an outgrowth of AEI's continuing research project in social and political processes.

We invited all major candidates for president, of both parties, to provide us with their views on nine issues that we consider of primary importance. We informed each of the candidates that we would publish their responses, unedited, in a book which we would then make available to the public. Each candidate was requested to limit his consideration of each issue to approximately two hundred words.

All of the invited candidates agreed to participate and sent us their responses.

The nine issues we asked the candidates to address emerged from a series of conferences held during AEI's annual Public Policy Week in mid-December 1979, in which we asked key policy makers and scholars to assess the challenges of the 1980s and to identify key issues.

The essays in this book will not only put the candidates on record on a wide variety of issues but will also assist AEI and the public in exploring various options available for major public policy problems. The questions we asked each candidate to address were:

How would you solve our nation's energy problems? Specifically, what would be the key elements of your national energy policy?

Most polls show that Americans consider inflation to be the number one domestic problem. How would you rid the economy of inflation?

The productivity growth rate of the American economy declined drastically in the 1970s. During 1979 it was negative. What steps would you take to restore productivity growth to the American economy? Do you believe we need to stimulate capital formation to aid in this? How would you do this?

Government regulation provides benefits, but it also imposes costs. What changes in the regulatory process, if any, would you propose?

In the last several years, there has been an increased concern with environmental protection. How would you achieve a balance between the need for economic growth and protection of the environment?

What should the United States stand for in world affairs in the 1980s? Concretely how would you propose that American ideals and interests prevail?

What would be the elements of your defense policy? How would you ensure the success of your vision of America's future in a changing and troubled world?

In recent years presidents of both parties have had great difficulty in getting Congress to adopt the programs they have recommended. What has caused this difficulty, and how would you go about overcoming it?

What policies or programs will you pursue that best reflect your sense of domestic priorities for the 1980s and beyond? What sacrifices will the American people be asked to make?

This volume exemplifies what is at the core of the American Enterprise Institute for Public Policy Research—that competition of ideas is fundamental to a free society. That competition of ideas we promote through the innovative research of our scholars, and through conferences and seminars and other forums in which varying viewpoints are brought together to meet the test of comparison. A companion principle is that public policy should be the policy of the public—that is, that equally strong as our dedication to competition in the market place of ideas is a similar commitment to the dissemination of ideas.

We have attempted to achieve part of this objective through the AEI associates program, a means of informing individuals and groups about innovative research and acquainting them with the various points of view on public policy issues. This program has several facets: an associates program for academia, a special seminar for chief executive officers, a series of management seminars for decision makers, a general associates program for the interested citizen.

Our goal with this volume is the same as with all activities of the institute: to enrich the debate on public policy and to disseminate varying viewpoints so that the full range of relevant options is explored and public policy is truly formed through the competition of ideas.

WILLIAM J. BAROODY, JR.
President, American Enterprise Institute

Contents

Anderson

JOHN B. ANDERSON has served since 1960 as a member from Illinois of the U.S. House of Representatives, where he is ranking Republican of the Rules of the House subcommittee of the House Rules Committee. For ten years, he chaired the House Republican Conference.

While with the Foreign Service, he acted as a staff adviser to the U.S. High Commissioner for Germany in West Berlin. Subsequently he was elected to three terms as state's attorney of Winnebago County, Ill. He is the author of *Between Two Worlds: A Congressman's Choice* and *Vision and Betrayal in America* and editor of *Congress and Conscience.* He received law degrees from the University of Illinois and Harvard University, after serving in the field artillery in World War II. He was born in 1922 in Rockford, Ill.

How would you solve our nation's energy problems? Specifically, what would be the key elements of your national energy policy?

In the six years since the Arab oil embargo and the quadrupling of world oil prices, the United States has steadfastly pursued a policy of energy "containment" by seeking to suppress domestic energy prices below an ever-growing—and ever more costly—dependence on foreign oil. Our energy "containment" policy has been an abject failure. We must now reverse that policy by decontrolling the pricing and allocation of our domestic energy supplies. It is not enough, however, to return to a "supply and demand" equilibrium in this country. With or without deregulation, OPEC will remain a power to be reckoned with in the decade ahead. Our oil import bill this year alone will rise to nearly $90 billion. We must stop this economic hemorrhage by accelerated conservation measures. I have proposed a gasoline tax (the proceeds of which could be refunded through payroll tax cuts, an increase in Social Security benefits, and a tax credit for business use of motor fuels) that could trim our annual gasoline consumption by as much as 700,000 barrels per day in the short run and substantially more in the long run, as motorists buy more fuel-efficient cars, switch to mass transit, and change their driving habits. Even greater savings are possible through residential and industrial conservation measures, if the government takes the initiative.

1

Most polls show that Americans consider inflation to be the number one domestic problem. How would you rid the economy of inflation?

Any program to deal with inflation necessarily involves an element of sacrifice. The unwillingness of the public and their elected representatives to make those sacrifices explains, no doubt, the failure of our recent endeavors. Sacrifice, in the form of fiscal restraint, must be the focal point of any antiinflationary stratagem. Continued reliance upon a monetary tourniquet to stem the hemorrhage of deficit spending invites recession and unduly penalizes small businessmen and other segments of our society. It must be understood, however, that fiscal restraint involves public sacrifice. Achieving a balanced budget will require us to forswear major new spending initiatives like national health insurance or the questionable MX missile system. It will require us to trim our more wasteful spending programs, particularly some of the categorical grant-in-aid programs like the Law Enforcement Assistance Administration. More importantly, it will require us to defer a general tax cut. A balanced budget, however, is not a cure-all. We must also boost our productivity by increasing savings and investment through selective tax cuts and boosting our R&D effort. Finally, we must come to grips with our ever more costly dependence on foreign oil. Here, too, an element of sacrifice is required. In the short term we must rely upon our most cost-effective energy option: conservation, or in more appropriate terms, enhancing our energy productivity.

The productivity growth rate of the American economy declined drastically in the 1970s. During 1979 it was negative. What steps would you take to restore productivity growth to the American economy? Do you believe we need to stimulate capital formation to aid in this? How would you do this?

Properly understood, capital formation is not a "business" concern, it is a very "human" concern. If we want an economy that is capable of producing 3 million jobs a year, if we want to reduce the incidence of poverty in this nation, if we want to provide a rising standard of living for all Americans, then we will have to promote greater capital formation. The capital formation issue must be treated in a broad, comprehensive fashion. First, we must boost the availability of capital by encouraging Americans at all levels to boost their savings and investment. I have suggested, for instance, that we ought to move gradually towards a $750 ($1,500 for married couples filing jointly) savings and dividend income exclusion. We must also take another look at the taxation of capital gains; the recent surge in inflation has largely neutralized the capital investment incentives contained in the 1978 law. Second, we must liberalize and simplify the existing tax depreciation allowances for capital assets. I favor the adoption of the 10-5-3 approach contained in the proposed Capital Cost Recovery Act. Finally, we must recognize the role that technology and R&D play in promoting capital expansion by boosting our R&D effort through tax incentives and the removal of regulatory impediments.

Government regulation provides benefits, but it also imposes costs. What changes in the regulatory process, if any, would you propose?

As my friend Murray Weidenbaum reminds me: *Beneficium invito non datur.* (A benefit cannot be bestowed on an unwilling person.)

The federal government should learn from that advice as it churns out regulatory dicta at unprecedented rates. Unless it does, the supposed beneficiaries of regulation will wonder if they are its victims instead.

Government must be able to separate the regulatory wheat from the regulatory chaff. To do so, the president and Congress must adopt specific approaches and plans for regulatory reform. I have introduced the Regulatory Reform Act to establish the procedural framework for systematic and comprehensive review of federal regulatory practices. Timetables would be set for presidential and congressional consideration of mandated regulatory reform plans. Several designated regulatory functions would be examined in each of several successive Congresses. Under this plan, both the president and Congress would have to act on the reform proposal to prevent legislative authority for the affected agency from terminating.

Government's regulatory appetite is fed, in part, by its propensity to grow larger and more interfering. If federal activities are to be reined in, limits must be placed on that appetite. To do this, I have advocated the "Limits of Government Act," which would peg federal spending to a percentage of our gross national product.

Both Congress and the president must share the blame for poor regulation just as much as they take credit for good regulation. Therefore, both must be part of the solution. My proposals serve this end by bringing both branches of government to bear on the problem.

In the last several years, there has been an increased concern with environmental protection. How would you achieve a balance between the need for economic growth and protection of the environment?

This point must be driven home: a good environment is good business. Since the onset of the Industrial Revolution, we have learned we can both utilize and husband our bountiful but limited resources. To promote the balance any good environmental policy needs, the federal government must use its strategic position to accommodate these different, and sometimes conflicting, interests.

No federal conservation policy or development program should proceed without accommodating environmental and developmental interests to the fullest extent possible. For instance, as a major sponsor of the Alaska Lands Act, I have acted to help ensure Alaska's continued economic development while preserving great sections of its wilderness.

Systematic and thoughtful consideration should be given to any environmental or developmental proposal; nothing should be railroaded into law. For example, I was an early proponent of an "Energy Mobilization Board" to expedite priority energy projects and cut through the layers of red tape at the local, state, and federal levels. Yet, any burgeoning synthetic fuels industry must be constrained from running roughshod over associated economic and environmental concerns.

I also would ensure that the burden of proving the wisdom and effectiveness of various environmental and developmental policies be shared by the government and those in the private sector making certain proposals. To illustrate, I have outlined a ten point nuclear energy plan which allows the continued development of nuclear energy contingent upon proof from government and the nuclear industry that operational and storage policies are safe and effective. Without these demonstrable assurances, nuclear development could not accelerate.

What should the United States stand for in world affairs in the 1980s? Concretely how would you propose that American ideals and interests prevail?

The United States should stand for peace, improvement in the standard of living for all people, and the pursuit of human rights for all peoples. While we should not shrink from military competition with the Soviet Union, our primary instruments to achieve our goals should be diplomatic, economic, political, and technological. We should rekindle the creative and innovative minds of our scientists and engineers who can tap the resources of space, earth, our oceans, and the human mind to provide services, technologies, and products to improve the quality of life for all. We should use the international airwaves to proclaim the benefits of our free enterprise system. We should use our capacity to feed the hungry and the poor to cement relations with the developing nations of the world. And, if necessary, we should demonstrate our will to use force to defend critical American interests abroad.

What would be the elements of your defense policy? How would you ensure the success of your vision of America's future in a changing and troubled world?

Several key elements, in addition to a strong, mobile military establishment, are necessary to preserve and enhance the security of our nation. First, we need a strong, innovative research and development community within and outside the government. Second, we need an intelligence community better able to identify threats and opportunities. Third, we need improved cooperation among our allies on defense, energy, economic, and other political areas of common interest. Fourth, we need to better insulate our economy from foreign interference with our energy and raw material supplies. Finally, we need to demonstrate both our willingness to cooperate with other nations in such diverse fields as arms control, science and technology, and cultural affairs and our willingness to compete in military forces, political propaganda, and economic matters. By demonstrating both our competitive and cooperative spirit through deed as well as word, I believe our nation will encourage international cooperation and be more secure in the long term.

In recent years presidents of both parties have had great difficulty in getting Congress to adopt the programs they have recommended. What has caused this difficulty, and how would you go about overcoming it?

After two years in office President Kennedy complained that a president could never get his own program through the Congress because Congress would always take it and make it its own. But therein lies the solution in overcoming difficulty in getting presidential programs through Congress—Congress must be persuaded that it has left its original mark on the legislation and that it will benefit both a majority of congressmen and their constituents.

While this seems an easy enough formula, the fact remains that in a democracy it involves considerable time and conflict. In the interim, the frustrated and impatient complain that the system has broken down, democracy is in deadlock, the president and Congress are at loggerheads, and America is lost. And yet, after nearly two centuries of this tug and pull between the president and Congress, periodically interspersed with stalemates and deadlocks of ominous proportions, the system is somehow still functioning and the Republic is as healthy and vibrant as ever. The reason: this is the way the Framers intended for our system to operate. They intentionally built in conflict between the two great branches, or, as Madison put it, "ambition must be made to counteract ambition," so that no one branch could completely dominate the other.

Today the president must be the chief legislative initiator, educator, persuader, and compromiser, but, if he is to ultimately succeed, he must also give Congress its proper due and deference through prior consultation and credit-giving on legislative initiatives. Conflict will continue to be inevitable, but a president can keep it both civil and creative.

What policies or programs will you pursue that best reflect your sense of domestic priorities for the 1980s and beyond? What sacrifices will the American people be asked to make?

While others may boast of their commitment to national health insurance, massive tax cuts, or large sustained increases in the defense budget, I am committed to the less glamorous alternative of fiscal restraint. With the economy reeling from double-digit inflation, I think it important for the nation to regain its fiscal balance. It will not be easy. The deficit for this fiscal year (FY 1980) is now estimated at $40 billion. The President has proposed a $16 billion deficit for fiscal year 1981, but even that seemingly significant reduction deficit is largely illusionary. The President's projected deficit does not incorporate an estimated $18 billion deficit in off-budget spending, nor $4–5 billion in on-budget supplemental fuel costs for the military. Other "savings" include $800 million from a hospital cost containment proposal already rejected by the House. Given the President's demonstrated optimism in fiscal matters, we can fully expect a deficit for 1981 in the neighborhood of $30 billion.

While others may boast of producing 1.5 million barrels per day of synthetic fuels by 1990, I am committed to energy deregulation and the conservation of an oil-equivalent of 4–5 million barrels per day by 1990 through conservation incentives in the transportation, residential, industrial, and commercial sectors.

Balancing the federal budget and reducing our dependence on foreign oil will require sacrifice from all Americans. We will have to defer tax cuts and spending initiatives. We will have to learn how to use less energy in our cars, our factories, and our homes. National sacrifice is not very alluring. The alternatives are even worse.

Baker

HOWARD H. BAKER, JR., has been a
Republican member of the U.S. Senate from
Tennessee since 1966 and minority leader
since 1977. He serves on the Foreign
Relations Committee, the Select Committee
on Intelligence, and the Environment and
Public Works Committee. In 1976, he was
appointed to the U.S. delegation to the
United Nations.

During World War II, Baker served in
the U.S. Navy as a PT boat commander. He
studied at Tulane University, the
University of the South, and the University
of Tennessee law school.

Before entering politics, Baker was an
attorney and businessman in Huntsville
and Knoxville in Tennessee. He was
born in Huntsville in 1925.

*How would you solve our nation's energy problems? Specifically,
what would be the key elements of your national energy policy?*

American production capabilities will get us out of the energy crisis
if we allow the market mechanism to operate free of oppressive
government regulation. We've got to establish a truly competitive
energy market which will promote the development of every possible
energy resource that we can muster.

Three years ago I recommended decontrol and deregulation of
oil and natural gas. I have also supported a windfall profits tax to
serve three purposes. First, to make sure that nobody "gouges" the
public. Second, to provide funds for research and development of new
energy systems and techniques to utilize every possible source of
energy. This would be of particular importance for the increased use
of our nation's abundant coal resources. Third, to cushion the impact
of increasing prices on those least able to afford it.

I think that coal is going to become an increasingly important
source of energy, and we must develop a coherent policy to encourage
its utilization throughout the nation. Conversion to coal-fired plants
has been unacceptably slow. I would also propose a quantum increase
in our conservation efforts. We ought to create an Energy Extension
Service, modeled after the Agricultural Extension Service, one of the
most successful government programs, to advise and counsel citizens
on how to maximize their energy conservation services.

7

We cannot abandon nuclear power, in spite of the difficulties we have encountered in building nuclear plants in a safe and socially acceptable way. To do so would amount to a loss of 10 percent of our current energy supplies. I would support the creation of a highly trained corps of nuclear engineers, modeled along the lines of the NASA astronaut training program, with nuclear plants built in segregated power parks located far away from population centers. We need a standard reactor that meets the most rigorous of performance and safety standards.

Most polls show that Americans consider inflation to be the number one domestic problem. How would you rid the economy of inflation?

No one can wave a magic wand and get rid of inflation. It took a while to get into this situation, and it will take us a while to dig ourselves out.

The first step must be the careful restraint of the spending policies of the federal government. The growth of federal spending must be slowed and then reduced. As president, I would use the veto power, if necessary, to achieve this goal.

We must provide real incentives for savings and investment, thereby making resources available for the improvement of economic productivity. A greater rate of investment in energy research and technology will also assist in solving the energy crisis which is playing havoc with our economic system.

A Baker administration would devise a comprehensive plan to dismantle regulations that impede competition and drive up costs and prices.

We must eliminate the counterproductive impact of the threat of wage and price controls. The prospect of such action invites people to hedge against it, either in setting prices, or negotiating long-term contracts for material, equipment, or labor. Controls and the threat thereof only exacerbate the market distortion which is at the core of our economic problems.

We must restrict the growth of the monetary supply until the inflation rate has been substantially reduced. The inadequate fiscal policies of the Carter administration have caused the Federal Reserve to monetize the debt with record high interest rates.

It is imperative that we formulate a schedule of tax cuts for various segments of the economy over the next four years. We must announce that schedule in advance and stick to it, thereby allowing the American wage earner and business executive to make spending, savings, and investment decisions with a degree of certainty.

The productivity growth rate of the American economy declined drastically in the 1970s. During 1979 it was negative. What steps would you take to restore productivity growth to the American economy? Do you believe we need to stimulate capital formation to aid in this? How would you do this?

I think that we have to remove the disincentives toward savings and investment which currently exist in the tax code.

One tax reform worthy of serious consideration is to switch from income taxes, corporate and personal, to a personal expenditure tax. This tax would look very similar to our current income taxes, but would allow a complete deduction for private savings. This personal expenditure tax would be preferable to an inherently regressive value-added tax.

In order to make the transition from the current tax system to an expenditure tax gradually, a series of interim proposals would make sense—for example, a universal IRA account in which anyone can make a deposit for retirement.

I would also recommend consideration of the gradual development and expansion of a tax exemption for interest income.

We must eliminate the false notion that, because a market may not work perfectly in some situations, that automatically means the government will do better. A less than perfect free market may well be better than a less than perfect government regulatory system.

An increased rate of government investment, and research and development expenditures, is long overdue. The share of government spending in these areas has fallen markedly in the last fifteen years. We need to expand both government and private investment, and government and private R&D expenditures, in order to expand technology and increase and modernize our capital stock. If we do not do so, we will not be able to compete effectively on world markets.

In my view, these changes and others would provide an enormous stimulation to capital formation and promote the long-term growth and increased productivity which is the core of our national strength.

Government regulation provides benefits, but it also imposes costs. What changes in the regulatory process, if any, would you propose?

Government regulation has become a serious impediment to economic growth in America. By some estimates, the cost of compliance with these regulations exceeds $100 billion a year—paid for in higher consumer prices and in a loss of productivity.

Standards for pollution control, job safety, and other social goals have undeniably contributed to an improvement in the quality of American life. Our air and water, for example, are cleaner today than they were ten years ago.

But in writing those laws, we foresaw a time when experience would show us where the costs of regulation exceeded any possible benefit. The time has now come for a comprehensive review of all such regulation, and for a careful revision of these regulations to meet the cost-benefit test which experience has provided.

While this review is undertaken, a moratorium on new regulations may well be in order. Such a review should not be seen as a retreat from high standards, but as a recognition that a more sophisticated approach to regulation is both possible and preferable.

A guiding principle of all regulatory policy should be to reject the false notion that simply because a market may not work perfectly in some circumstances, government will automatically do better. The last forty-five years have provided abundant examples of the error in this assumption, and we will ignore those lessons at our economic peril.

In the last several years, there has been an increased concern with environmental protection. How would you achieve a balance between the need for economic growth and protection of the environment?

In the 1970s, this nation made a commitment to a clean environment. I supported that commitment as a member of the Senate Environment and Public Works Committee. I was a coauthor of the Clean Water Act, the Clean Air Act, the Safe Drinking Water Act, the Solid Waste Act, and many others. I am proud of my environmental record.

The key word to remember is balance. When we passed that original legislation, we provided for follow-up review and revisions. We were well aware that we were writing on a blank slate and that some of our actions would go too far, and some would not go far enough. By providing for later review, we hoped to build in a certain degree of flexibility.

The value of a clean environment is clearly difficult to quantify, but a stable, clean environment is a valuable and worthwhile goal, and I do not intend to abandon it.

Industry has supported these goals and has achieved fantastic success. More than 90 percent of American industry has met its environmental standards.

Some environmental regulations have failed to require a conscious balancing of costs and benefits. In cases where enormous investments are required without a deliberate effort to evaluate benefits, those requirements encounter difficulty in obtaining respect from the business community and others who must bear the cost.

This is particularly true for the marginal incremental improvement. For example, it may be possible to remove 95 percent of pollution from a particular source for a certain number of dollars. However, to remove that remaining 5 percent of the pollution often requires an astronomical increase in the cost of compliance.

In addition, certain environmental statutes have disregarded the practicalities of implementation. These statutes generate needless friction and controversy by failing to allow for adequate time to phase in new requirements. While this is not true of all regulations, such instances fuel a general sense of dissatisfaction with government regulatory programs.

The current legislative and regulatory framework reflects a noble and worthwhile experiment. With the advent of new information, technology, and experience, we must now modify the experiment to maximize its productive value. Far from weakening the environmental movement, such a modification and increased sophistication can only strengthen it.

What should the United States stand for in world affairs in the 1980s? Concretely how would you propose that American ideals and interests prevail?

We believe in life. We believe in liberty. We believe in the pursuit of happiness. We did not claim these rights for ourselves alone, but for all mankind: for the starving child in Cambodia, for the refugee in Palestine, for the artist in Russia, for the Catholic who lives in Poland, and for the Jew who died there.

It is the strength of these beliefs, and our commitment to them in the face of all challenge, which has made America something special in the world.

More than once we have paid a heavy price for our commitment. We believed with Woodrow Wilson that "the right is more precious than peace," and we agreed with Franklin D. Roosevelt that "we are willing to fight to maintain freedom."

Though we are slow to anger, we have fought. Though born to comfort, we have suffered and died in the defense of ideals. Freedom and justice are, to us, more than words. They are the fundamental rights of man.

It is our commitment to justice—not to narrow self-interest—which has gained us the trust of nations locked in ancient, mortal conflict, and which has brought them together at the table of peace.

It is our commitment to freedom which leads me to bear the heavy burden of armaments until the day when peace is something more than the mere absence of war.

But whatever burden we must bear, the world should know that the United States has not lost its appetite for leadership, that there are still some things we will always stand for and some things we will never stand for.

What would be the elements of your defense policy? How would you ensure the success of your vision of America's future in a changing and troubled world?

The United States must resolve above all else to defend itself and protect its interests in this world—not simply for our own safety and security, not only to guarantee the peace, but also to ensure that civilization itself will survive on this planet.

We must establish a credible deterrent to any potential aggressor at every level of potential conflict, for it is only in that deterrence that any reasonable hope for peace and security can be found.

At the conventional level, this means having enough troops, ships, planes, ammunition, enough quality, and enough pride to project our power effectively and confidently to crisis points around the world.

Across the dread threshold of nuclear war, deterrence means having enough missiles, bombers, warning and control systems, and protection—for ourselves and our allies—to survive a nuclear attack and strike a devastating blow in return.

In none of these requirements is our strength sufficient today. We must rebuild our forces, encourage our allies to bear greater responsibility for their home defense, and negotiate an arms limitation agreement that will truly limit and perhaps reduce the capacity for violence on this planet.

In recent years presidents of both parties have had great difficulty in getting Congress to adopt the programs they have recommended. What has caused this difficulty, and how would you go about overcoming it?

Presidents of the recent past have failed in the process of their decision making to incorporate the congressional perspective. When the system works effectively, the Congress *and* the president govern; either they act in tandem or they do not act successfully at all.

My entire public life has been spent in the observation of and participation in the interaction between the White House and the Congress. I have seen first hand the achievements of a cooperative

White House–congressional relationship and the disappointments and failures of antagonism.

My own experience in the Senate as Republican leader has equipped me with the skills to bring the key participants together to act constructively and provide a unified vision which encompasses their views in a coherent and politically acceptable fashion. In my opinion, that is the essence of leadership.

It is not enough to identify the problems and suggest solutions. One must be able to convince the country and its representatives to follow.

I have brought this ability to the United States Senate, and I intend to bring it to the White House.

What policies or programs will you pursue that best reflect your sense of domestic priorities for the 1980s and beyond? What sacrifices will the American people be asked to make?

Domestic priorities for the 1980s will focus on our economic problems. Our major dilemmas are no longer unemployment and inadequate social programs but rather inflation, excessive growth of government, and sluggish economic growth.

These are problems not just for the wealthy, or the general populace, but for the poor as well. The ability of minorities, women, and the poor to experience upward social and economic mobility will be maximized in a noninflationary, growing economy and minimized in an economy of high inflation and sluggish growth.

Not only will the general tax-paying working population be less willing to share (through government taxes and government transfer payment programs) its wealth with the less fortunate in an economy which is growing too slowly, but the direct benefit of economic opportunity in a rapidly growing economy will be much less available to these groups if our current policies and economic performance continue.

Every year that we delay starting on the road to a more sensible budgetary, tax, monetary, and regulatory policy is at least another year before we reap the eventual benefits of such a policy.

I strongly believe that a political coalition can be forged which will recognize the advantages to all of our citizens of making noninflationary growth our highest priority even if it means temporary economic sacrifices and putting aside our debates over the division of a static GNP.

Brown

EDMUND G. BROWN, JR., has served as the governor of California since 1975. In 1969 he was elected to the Los Angeles Community College Board of Trustees, and in 1970 he was the only Democrat elected to a partisan state constitutional office. Brown served as California's secretary of state from 1971 to 1975.

Before he became active in politics, Brown worked as a research attorney for the California Supreme Court and for a Los Angeles law firm. He received his law degree from Yale in 1964, and he graduated from the University of California at Berkeley in 1961. He also attended the University of Santa Clara and studied for the priesthood at Sacred Heart Novitiate, in Los Gatos, California. He was born in 1938 in San Francisco.

How would you solve our nation's energy problems? Specifically, what would be the key elements of your national energy policy?

We must develop our own energy sources and cut waste if we are to become self-reliant. First, a mandatory gasoline rationing program would curb consumption and bring home to the American people the seriousness of our dependence on foreign oil. In addition, there must be a significant expansion of conservation in all sectors of the economy. We must boost domestic energy sources, particularly the use of solar, cogeneration, biomass, hydro, wind, and geothermal energy and coal. We must also recognize that our own domestic inflation is intimately connected with price increases by OPEC. The present system of demanding more foreign oil for continuously eroding dollar assets is not a viable long-term policy. It will result in lower production by OPEC and unacceptable price increases. By negotiating for oil imports on a government-to-government basis, we can link the reduction of our own domestic inflation with the stabilization of oil prices. I would also work to create closer cooperation with Canada and Mexico on the energy front and would favor formation of a North American Economic Community.

14

Most polls show that Americans consider inflation to be the number one domestic problem. How would you rid the economy of inflation?

I am convinced that the direction of the country must change. Productivity rates are declining, the dollar is weaker, inflation is almost beyond control, and the situation abroad is becoming increasingly unstable. But instead of seeking to rebuild our strength, the leadership in Washington continues to offer more government programs, more budget deficits, more basic weakness. Simply by continuing to print more money, the Carter administration and Congress can, in effect, kid the American people that hard choices don't have to be made. Therefore, I would support the balanced budget amendment that is now pending before the Senate Judiciary Committee. I would place a freeze on federal employment and would allow no new programs to be added to the budget until other programs are trimmed. In the long run, I want to control inflation by shifting this country from an era of excess consumption, fueled by public and private debt, to an era of investment in our environmental, technological, and human assets.

The productivity growth rate of the American economy declined drastically in the 1970s. During 1979 it was negative. What steps would you take to restore productivity growth to the American economy? Do you believe we need to stimulate capital formation to aid in this? How would you do this?

We cannot continue to perpetuate the myths of the 1950s and 1960s by inflating our economy with deficit spending. Instead of more government programs, we must encourage investment—through tax incentives and selective assistance—to rebuild this nation's industrial base and stimulate new technology. We must shift the ethic, the attitude of this country from borrowing and consuming to saving and investing. In my campaign I have called for a reindustrialization of our society, a move away from planned obsolescence and waste to greater efficiency, conservation, and stewardship. Our country has both the people and the resources. We must mobilize them by retooling, rebuilding, and reequipping this nation so that we can compete during the 1980s. I am confident that our leadership in agriculture, in electronics, in aerospace, and in a host of other industries can be enhanced and can form the basis for a renewed long-term productivity. But we have to wake up this country. We have to wake up to the fact that we are facing the turn in the road. The complacency, the smug games that are being played in Washington are not going to make it in the 1980s.

Government regulation provides benefits, but it also imposes costs. What changes in the regulatory process, if any, would you propose?

There is no question that government regulations, like those of any private or public bureaucracy, have sometimes gotten out of hand in the past decade. I favor elimination of unnecessarily burdensome regulation, especially for small businesses, on a case-by-case basis. At the same time, it is a mistake to fail to acknowledge the serious problems that have given birth to the need for government regulation. I strongly favor the *process* of government regulation in such areas as providing competitive fares and service in the trucking industry, greater control of the more than 70,000 toxic substances which threaten our biosphere, and even *stronger* quality standards on substances so basic to life as air and water. It should also be remembered that pollution control itself provides jobs, and health-care costs engendered in part by industrial pollution have their own price tag.

In the last several years, there has been an increased concern with environmental protection. How would you achieve a balance between the need for economic growth and protection of the environment?

This country can have economic growth and protect the environment if we do a better job of allocating our national product. I think the public sector will have to take a more advanced role in selecting out those industries that are capable of productivity increases and are relevant to our needs. Much like the Japanese and German experience, this will involve a new compact with labor, business, environmentalists, and consumers. I see such an alliance as giving us the productivity to provide for people's needs. I think people want mobility. They want more information. They want the good life. But unless we can rebuild our dominant technologies, unless we can train those who are left untrained, and unless we can protect our soils and our forests and our air and our water, we're not going to get those things. By drawing upon an increasingly aging and inefficient industrial base, we will end up with increasing pollution and economic decline. The only way out is a fiscal and monetary policy that fosters saving and investment to generate the necessary capital.

What should the United States stand for in world affairs in the 1980s? Concretely how would you propose that American ideals and interests prevail?

The world has changed profoundly during the last twenty-five years as 100 new countries have come into the family of nations. Many of them have become strong and productive. As a result, we should no longer try to maintain the role of policeman of the free world. We need as part of our foreign policy a recognition that the time has come to demand of our allies and of other nations that they assume greater responsibility for their own defense and vital interests. A president has to understand this new role and explain it to the American people. We should look on this new approach as a constructive development and encourage regional groupings of nations to act for their common defense, allowing America to provide its greater strength and technology and military capacity in a partnership fashion. Whatever actions we take, they should be guided by our fundamental commitment to freedom and self-determination.

What would be the elements of your defense policy? How would you ensure the success of your vision of America's future in a changing and troubled world?

The first element of a sound defense policy is a robust domestic economy. We need to reindustrialize in the 1980s, encouraging productivity and investment as part of a comprehensive North American strategy to rebuild our economic base. Secondly, we need to enter into mutual defense *partnerships* with our major allies in Europe, Japan, and the Middle East. The United States can no longer afford to guarantee the world's security as a sort of global policeman. Thirdly, we need to pursue realistic arms control and a mutuality of interest among superpowers, resisting jingoistic pressures to mindlessly step up the cold war. Such a defense policy will make us strong enough to promote a vision of global cooperation where possible and political nonmilitary competition where necessary.

In recent years presidents of both parties have had great difficulty in getting Congress to adopt the programs they have recommended. What has caused this difficulty, and how would you go about overcoming it?

I recognize the difficulty between the executive branch and the Congress. I don't think that's a new phenomenon. I think it existed under Ford, it existed under Nixon, it existed under Kennedy in the early 1960s. It's part of what I see as an unwinding of American concepts that, while viable in the post–World War II period, are now becoming unworkable. And we're going through a period in which there is not a strong unity, or what I would call a governing coalition. The Democratic party is falling apart, in my judgment. There is no easy road.

There is no one personality who is going to change that. I would rather see the building of a new coalition based not just on the eloquence of a new leader, but on the redefinition of America's role in the world, of a more enlightened approach to our own reindustrialization and the building of a coalition based on that; and then, through that process, developing the ability to bring about decisive action.

What policies or programs will you pursue that best reflect your sense of domestic priorities for the 1980s and beyond? What sacrifices will the American people be asked to make?

My basic perspective is one that looks to the future. I see a global politics emerging out of the need to develop the planet without destroying it. But I don't think in America we have focused enough on the consequences of what we are doing now and how those actions will impact on the year 2000. With respect to energy, environment, nuclear power, training of minorities, the rebuilding of our cities, we need much tougher policies to get us over the hurdle of impending stagnation, where I see us now moving. The president must explain this situation to the people and make clear the kinds of sacrifice and commitment that will be necessary to pull America out of its malaise and raise it to new levels of greatness. The decade ahead will require discipline, frugality, and conservation. If new initiatives are going to be embarked on, some of the old ones are going to have to be curtailed. That is what I describe as the "era of limits." Put simply, to get more investment, we must have less consumption and more saving.

Bush

GEORGE BUSH was director of the Central Intelligence Agency in 1976–1977 and U.S. ambassador to the United Nations in 1971–1973. He was a member of the U.S. House of Representatives from Texas from 1966 to 1970.

Bush served as chairman of the Republican National Committee, 1973–1974. In 1974–1975, he was chief, U.S. Liaison Office, People's Republic of China.

Bush was a U.S. Navy carrier pilot in the Pacific during World War II. He graduated from Yale University. Before election to Congress, he was president of Zapata Off-Shore Company, an oil-drilling equipment firm in Houston. He was born in Milton, Mass., in 1924.

How would you solve our nation's energy problems? Specifically, what would be the key elements of your national energy policy?

Our fundamental, long-term problem in the United States is not so much a lack of energy but a surplus of government.

More than a quarter of a century ago, Washington embarked upon a policy of artificially holding down energy prices in order to protect consumers. But it was a policy that came more from the heart than the head, for over time, it helped to create a host of problems—it drove up consumption; it drove down production; and then, as we were gradually caught in the coils of OPEC, it accelerated the drain on our dollars and made us dangerously dependent on foreign oil sources. Now, consumers are paying a heavy price in rapidly escalating energy bills and our president speaks of war in order to protect the oil lanes.

I intend to change these policies. As president, I will seek to restore the forces of the marketplace through immediate decontrol of oil and gas. I am opposed to dramatically higher gasoline taxes until we first give the free market a chance to work. To ensure that the proceeds from the marketplace are invested in new sources of energy, I will seek a plow-back—energy reinvestment—provision as part of a windfall profits tax. I will seek to remove the legislative and bureaucratic roadblocks to coal production and move immediately to get both our electric generating plants and our manufacturers off the foreign oil habit—and onto coal and nuclear power. I will support tax incentives for conservation. And I will correct the incredible failure of the Carter administration to create a working strategic petroleum reserve—our most effective insurance against oil blackmail.

These policy changes will move us toward energy security and economic strength, but they will not solve the long-term energy challenges. To do that, we must develop and bring together the best minds and the financial resources of the free world—energy-producing and consuming nations alike—to demonstrate and perfect safe, clean, and reliable new energy resources by the year 2000.

The energy future is ours if we have the wisdom and strength to reverse the errors of the past.

Most polls show that Americans consider inflation to be the number one domestic problem. How would you rid the economy of inflation?

Three years of Carternomics have been devastating for America. Inflation last year was three times what it was when this administration was elected—and, in fact, hit the highest level in more than thirty years. Purchasing power last year declined by 5.3 percent; interest rates and home prices hit record highs, and savings rates hit record lows.

Tragically, this administration seems paralyzed in the face of adversity. Its new economic forecast calls for yet another year of double-digit inflation, and its new budget calls for yet another massive increase in taxes.

The Carter administration falsely proclaims that all of our problems are rooted in OPEC price increases; they are *not*. Weak leadership, in Washington, is at the heart of our problem.

It is time to abandon the counsel of despair that we hear from the White House and to find a new counsel of hope. If we act wisely—on energy and on inflation—we have it within our power to conquer both problems together and emerge as a great and resilient people once again.

We can and we will bring inflation under control if we adopt a coordinated program to:

• balance the federal budget by controlling spending and limiting the growth of government

• revitalize the economy through supply-side tax cuts to generate jobs, encourage savings, investment, and energy efficiency

• reduce the crushing tax burden for American taxpayers

• prune the thicket of conflicting and redundant regulations and laws that stifle creativity, economic growth, and productive investment.

The fundamental economic facts are simple. It is time for the government to face up to them. I am committed to ensuring that we do so.

The productivity growth rate of the American economy declined drastically in the 1970s. During 1979 it was negative. What steps would you take to restore productivity growth to the American economy? Do you believe we need to stimulate capital formation to aid in this? How would you do this?

Economists now confess that many of the old rules of their profession no longer seem to work in today's world, but there is one rule that is still irrefutable: rising productivity is the key to a rising standard of living.

In the quarter century after World War II, productivity in the United States rose at about 3 percent a year and Americans enjoyed the greatest surge of prosperity in our history. In the 1970s, productivity growth was cut in half and then in half again—and incomes went into a stall. Then in 1979, productivity growth actually dipped into negative figures—and income fell.

As U.S. productivity during the 1970s dropped to the lowest level of all the major industrialized democracies, many of our most important industries—autos, steel, textiles, etc.—also came under enormous competitive pressure.

Clearly, one of our overriding tasks in the 1980s is to restore the vigor and vitality of our economy:

• We must pursue disciplined fiscal and monetary policies to halt the inflation that is so severely inhibiting capital formation.

• We must overhaul the tax laws that now penalize savings and investment. Rules governing depreciation, expensing of research and development, and credit for job training—all must be reformed.

• And we must lift the regulation burden that is now retarding innovation and causing great waste and inefficiency.

The Carter administration has had three years to wrestle with these issues, and the record shows that the problems have only grown worse. It's time for a change.

Government regulation provides benefits, but it also imposes costs. What changes in the regulatory process, if any, would you propose?

The analytical case against excessive regulation is now abundantly established; what remains to be done is to elect an administration that pays more than lip service to it.

Clearly, the Carter administration fails that test. Some progress has indeed been made in the area of airline reform, but for every step forward, there have been dozens of others in the wrong direction. The avalanche of more than fifty thousand pages of new regulations every year, the creation of a mammoth new energy bureaucracy, the imposition of a Rube Goldberg system of wage-price guidelines—all bespeak of a lack of serious commitment by those now in charge.

I am committed to a fundamentally different program:

• to the removal of all regulators who have lost faith in private enterprise and to their replacement by men and women who have a more balanced and knowledgeable view of the nation's economic needs

• to repeal of those regulations that are stifling growth and to the simplification of others that are creating enormous waste and inefficiency

• to greater experimentation and reliance upon market incentive (pollution taxes, for example) in place of bureaucratic dictates from Washington

• to rigorous cost-benefit analysis of new regulations

• to a more serious investigation of "regulatory budgets"

• and finally, to the introduction of a new spirit in Washington: a spirit that says we will once again build a great nation when we once again limit the powers of government and expand the freedoms of our people.

In the last several years, there has been an increased concern with environmental protection. How would you achieve a balance between the need for economic growth and protection of the environment?

In many ways, our struggle to preserve the environment is now in mid-passage.

Nearly two decades have passed since Rachel Carson's book, *Silent Spring*, propelled the nation into action, and during that time, considerable progress has been made. We should be proud that the air over some of our great cities like New York and Los Angeles is cleaner today and the water in many of our rivers and lakes is purer than twenty years ago.

Yet, we have also come to recognize over time that some of our environmental rules have imposed high costs upon our economy without compensating benefits. One of the first tasks of a new administration should be a thorough review of all laws and regulations in this area so that we can make mid-course corrections.

I reject the notion that we must sacrifice either economic growth or environmental progress. Such a cramped view of the future is neither worthy of our heritage nor is it justified by our awesome capabilities in science and technology. We just have to keep working at it.

22

At the same time, we must recognize that in the 1980s, new priorities have also arisen. We must now face up to the difficult tasks of controlling highly toxic chemicals in the workplace and the general environment, and we must evaluate and meet potential threats to the global ecology, such as acid rain.

The story of the Love Canal was personally appalling to me. I am determined that during a Bush administration, the nation will squarely address this question of safe disposal of hazardous wastes.

What should the United States stand for in world affairs in the 1980s? Concretely how would you propose that American ideals and interests prevail?

When I worked in China as U.S. representative there, one of the first things I learned was that in writing the word "crisis" the Chinese join together two other symbols—one standing for "danger," the other for "opportunity."

That is very much the way I see the world today. We are now on the threshold of a dangerous decade for America. Our strategic forces are more vulnerable than at any time in our history, our nation is extraordinarily dependent on OPEC oil, our alliances are frayed, and the Soviets are on the march.

Clearly, this is a time of peril. But with courage and creativity, it can also be a time of opportunity for America:

• We can seize this opportunity to finally repair our military forces by reversing the do-nothing policies that have characterized the Carter administration for so long.

• We can seize this opportunity to free ourselves from foreign oil by removing governmental controls over our own producers and stepping up our conservation efforts.

• And we can seize this opportunity to rebuild our relationships with others by forging a new set of partnerships based upon shared interests in defense, energy, and economic matters. Instead of beating old friends over the head because we disagree with their internal policies, we should work with them to advance mutual goals—and in the process, we will serve the cause of human freedom everywhere.

Carterism has failed because it has neither had a coherent sense of what it wants nor the discipline to stick to what it says. This "splendid oscillation" has left us where we are today.

By adopting a new course—a course that we follow steadily and consistently—I am convinced that we can ease the Russian bear back in his cage and create once again a more peaceful world.

What would be the elements of your defense policy? How would you ensure the success of your vision of America's future in a changing and troubled world?

Two critical questions now confront us in national defense. First, how can we best restore our military strength? Second, who is best qualified to serve as our commander in chief during perilous times?

Fortunately, the country has finally woken up to the fact that we are entering a decade of great danger. For the first time in our history, our strategic forces will be seriously vulnerable to Soviet attack and our conventional forces will be inferior. Events in Afghanistan should also leave no doubt that the Russians will take advantage of weakness wherever they find it.

It is thus obvious that we must press forward with a sustained build-up of our forces. Among our highest priorities should be the development and deployment of a new manned bomber, a long-range cruise missile, a greatly strengthened, three-ocean navy, and expanded airborne and seaborne tactical forces.

I also support draft registration for both men and women, and I would like to see an immediate investigation of the readiness of our military troops. If the facts demand it, we should not hesitate to increase financial incentives for those in uniform or even to return to the draft. I am confident that our young people will rally to the flag as the need is there.

These changes may cost money—more than is called for in the administration's new budget. But we can no longer afford policies built more on bluff than true brawn.

In my view, Mr. Carter has proven himself unfit to continue as commander in chief. Over the past three years, in the face of a massive Soviet build-up, he cut nearly $40 billion from the projected defense budgets of President Ford. One weapons system after another has been delayed or cancelled.

Even his recent conversion to higher spending was wrung from him only as a concession in order to win approval of the SALT Treaty. We should not be taken in by a sheep in wolves' clothing.

In recent years presidents of both parties have had great difficulty in getting Congress to adopt the programs they have recommended. What has caused this difficulty, and how would you go about overcoming it?

The failure of the Carter administration to achieve many of its most cherished goals in Congress—SALT II is only the most recent example—has also exploded a popular myth. No longer need anyone believe that simply having a president and a Congress from the same political party guarantees national progress.

What counts far more is the quality of the relationship between the White House and Capitol Hill. Even to this day, many congressmen regard Mr. Carter as distant and inaccessible, and the administration has proved unable to build a smooth, cooperative relationship with the leadership.

I believe I can do better than that. In recent years, I have been privileged to spend four years in the House as a member of the Ways and Means Committee, and I have also had the opportunity to serve in the executive branch.

From that service, I not only acquired a working knowledge of Washington but established many of my closest friendships—and, I might add, on both sides of the aisle. It has been heartening to me that one of the nation's finest members of Congress, Barber Conable, is chairman of my national steering committee; several other members have stumped for me on the campaign trail; and in polls of the GOP delegation in Congress, I have consistently won their vote as their first choice for the presidency.

Personal friendships are not the whole answer, of course. A president must also enunciate clear, firm policies—policies that he sticks to day-in, day-out, unlike the Carter administration. But by building on the base that I now have and by offering firm, decisive leadership from the White House, I believe that cooperation can be established, that a consensus can be built—and that the nation can finally move ahead again in unity.

What policies or programs will you pursue that best reflect your sense of domestic priorities for the 1980s and beyond? What sacrifices will the American people be asked to make?

As we head into the eighties, we face many needs here at home—to renew the bonds of family and of neighborhood, to reverse the deterioration in our public schools, to rebuild many of our cities, to strengthen our transportation system, to rebuild our housing stock, etc. There can be no doubt, however, that our highest domestic concern should be inflation.

The 13 percent inflation we experienced last year was not only the highest in over three decades, but it is rippling through our entire economy with devastating consequences. Falling standards of living, falling productivity, falling savings rates, and falling confidence in democracy itself—all of these and more are the price we pay for runaway inflation.

This dragon has so many heads that we must attack everywhere at once. The federal budget must be balanced at long last, waste must be cut, tax laws must be revised to stimulate savings and investment, the regulatory burden must be eased, and the energy industry must be freed from interventionist governmental policies.

One reason for our inflation is that we are placing too many demands upon our limited resources. To conquer inflation, then, we must reduce some of those demands and postpone others. Some may say that is too high a sacrifice; but I believe the vast majority of Americans are prepared to take whatever steps are necessary to put this nation back on the road to economic sanity.

Carter

JIMMY CARTER was elected the thirty-ninth president of the United States in 1976.

After taking the naval ROTC program at Georgia Institute of Technology, he went on to the U.S. Naval Academy, graduating in 1946, and did postgraduate work at Union College, in Schenectady, N.Y. He was assigned to the nuclear submarine program.

Following the death of his father in 1953, he resigned his naval commission and returned to Plains, Ga., to manage his family's farm and peanut warehouse, subsequently starting a fertilizer and seed business. He was elected to the Georgia Senate in 1962 and in 1970 was elected governor of Georgia. In 1973 he became the Democratic party's national chairman for the next year's elections.

President Carter's autobiography *Why Not the Best?* was published in 1975. He was born in 1924 in Plains.

How would you solve our nation's energy problems? Specifically, what would be the key elements of your national energy policy?

The President has warned repeatedly that the United States is dangerously dependent on imported oil, much of it controlled by OPEC. The American people are responding with increasing involvement in conservation programs—the keystone of any successful energy effort. President Carter is confident that the Congress also will respond.

The President is calling upon the Congress to adopt his remaining legislative priorities so that the United States has a compact, far-reaching energy program. These priorities are (1) passage of the windfall profits tax on the oil industry, with the funds being used to help in achieving our energy independence goals; (2) establishment of an Energy Mobilization Board, which would eliminate unnecessary red tape in the construction of needed energy facilities; (3) creation of the Energy Security Corporation, enabling us to finance a massive program to develop alternative energy fuels; (4) adoption of a utility oil use reduction program, requiring utilities to substantially convert from oil to coal-burning or other energy facilities over a defined timetable; and (5) adoption of a standby gasoline rationing plan, which will prepare us for any significant energy supply interruption. The President also believes that a key element of any energy program must be movement to a realistic pricing policy. This is one reason for the decision to decontrol prices. It is important that the American people not be fooled into believing that energy is cheap.

The President is confident that our security and our freedom will not be auctioned off for foreign oil.

Most polls show that Americans consider inflation to be the number one domestic problem. How would you rid the economy of inflation?

This inflation took fifteen years to build up; it cannot be eliminated overnight. The administration's antiinflation program was designed to cope with the very special inflation factors confronting our nation. So far, double-digit price increases have been heavily concentrated in the areas of energy and housing. In the short term the goal of antiinflation policy must be to "quarantine" these increases and prevent them from spilling over into the basic wage-price structure of our economy. This calls for public restraint—in the form of a tight budget and restrained monetary policy—and private restraint.

This program has been successful in the face of very difficult circumstances. Increases in 1979 compensation did not increase any faster than in 1978—despite very high energy inflation. The President has submitted a tight budget for fiscal year 1981. Continued cooperation with wage and price guidelines is essential.

Over the longer term the President believes this nation must address the structural problems that create and drive inflation. This means increasing productivity and freeing resources for private use—which the President has begun in submitting a tight budget for fiscal 1981; this means reducing the burden of excess regulation— which the President has done with his regulatory reform program. It also means reducing our vulnerability to outside shocks. The administration's grain reserve program protects the U.S. economy from sudden price increases caused by a worldwide crop failure. And, most importantly, the President's energy program is designed to loosen the hold OPEC has on our economy.

The productivity growth rate of the American economy declined drastically in the 1970s. During 1979 it was negative. What steps would you take to restore productivity growth to the American economy? Do you believe we need to stimulate capital formation to aid in this? How would you do this?

When President Carter established the National Productivity Council in 1978, he stated that improvement in the growth of productivity is essential to the social and economic welfare of the American people. Three months ago he announced the administration's industrial innovation initiatives which will help boost our nation's productivity. The steps include the establishment of a special center within the National Technical Information Service to improve the flow of knowledge from federal laboratories and research and development centers so industries can be better informed of technological opportunities.

Other steps are the strengthening of the federal government's capacity to provide domestic industries with information on foreign research and development activities.

The President also proposed several specific steps to increase technical knowledge through establishment of such activities as nonprofit centers at universities or other private sector sites to develop and transfer generic technologies—that is, technologies that underlie industrial sectors such as welding and joining, robotics, corrosion prevention and control.

The President's program further includes strengthening our patent system, clarification of antitrust policy, and placing special emphasis on encouraging the development of small innovative firms. Improvements in productivity also require increased investment. The Revenue Act of 1978, approved by the President, allocated a larger than normal share of the tax reductions to corporate tax reduction—including a change in the capital gains tax. The President's anti-inflation program helps—economic stability has a positive effect on investment. And when the economic situation allows for a tax cut in the 1980s, this administration will look to cuts that increase productivity without stimulating inflation.

Government regulation provides benefits, but it also imposes costs. What changes in the regulatory process, if any, would you propose?

In his 1980 State of the Union Message, President Carter wrote:

> In March of 1979, I sent to Congress the Regulation Reform Act. When enacted, this bill will assure that new and existing regulations will be rigorously scrutinized before they can be issued or retained, that wasteful delays are eliminated from the regulatory process, that key regulatory officials be selected purely on grounds of integrity and competence, and that the public will be assured meaningful opportunities to participate in regulatory decision-making. The reform steps I have taken administratively have already avoided billions of dollars in unnecessary regulatory costs, erased thousands of useless regulations from the books of OSHA and other

agencies, and opened up the regulatory process across the Executive Branch. Enactment of my regulatory reform bill legislation is needed in this Congress, to strengthen these regulatory commissions.

In the last several years, there has been an increased concern with environmental protection. How would you achieve a balance between the need for economic growth and protection of the environment?

In President Carter's opinion, economic growth and environmental protection are not incompatible. In fact, if our major indicators of economic growth took proper account of improvements in environmental quality—which people value highly but which are not "bought" and "sold" in the same way other goods and services are— carefully crafted environmental regulations would be seen as a boon to economic growth. There is no benefit seen in permitting the uncontrolled pollution of air and water or the unchecked disposal of hazardous wastes. Where this has occurred, damages have generally far exceeded what we would have had to spend to prevent them.

Energy conservation also illustrates the harmony of economic growth and environmental protection—not only does it make good economic sense, but it also lessens the need to develop new energy sources that may be risky, environmentally disruptive, or both. However, the President believes that environmental and other regulations can be improved.

Indeed, the goal of the President's Regulatory Reform Act—repeated in the State of the Union address—is to ensure that we meet our environmental and other goals in the least expensive way possible. Toward this end, the Environmental Protection Agency's new "bubble" policy makes industry a partner in environmental protection and allows them, and us, to save money on pollution control while at the same time holding to the high standards of environmental quality that the citizens of this nation clearly desire. In this and other ways, we can protect our environment and resource heritage while at the same time providing an economic climate that can improve the material well-being of all Americans.

What should the United States stand for in world affairs in the 1980s? Concretely how would you propose that American ideals and interests prevail?

President Carter is determined that the United States remain the strongest of all nations—economically, morally, ethically, and militarily. This continued strength is necessary if the United States is to be a beacon for other nations to follow.

In his State of the Union address, the President outlined several steps the United States will take so that American ideals and interests prevail. He said: "We can thrive in a world of change if we remain true to our values and actively engaged in promoting world peace."

The paths taken by the United States in the next decade will include continuing to work for peace in the Middle East and Southern Africa, working with our allies to protect our vital interests in the Persian Gulf, continuing to build our ties with developing nations and respecting and helping to strengthen their national independence, and continuing our commitment to support the growth of democracy and the protection of human rights.

The President has pointed out that "we must face the world as it is," and this includes the continued competition with the Soviet Union. The Soviet invasion of Afghanistan, for example, is a key example of the need to maintain our readiness.

Regarding what he expects will be a decade of rapid change, the President said: "But America need have no fear. We can thrive in a world of change if we remain true to our values and actively engaged in promoting world peace."

What would be the elements of your defense policy? How would you ensure the success of your vision of America's future in a changing and troubled world?

Since taking office, the President has sustained annual real growth in defense spending, necessary to overcome the many years of declining real defense budgets in the late 1960s and 1970s.

The President's defense program emphasizes these areas: (1) ensuring that our strategic nuclear forces will be equivalent to those of the Soviet Union and capable of deterring any nuclear aggression; (2) upgrading our forces so the military balance between NATO and the Warsaw Pact will continue to deter the outbreak of war; (3) providing forces to give us the ability to come quickly to the aid of friends and allies around the globe; and (4) ensuring that our Navy continues to be the world's most powerful. This program includes the cruise missile production to modernize our strategic air deterrent, B-52 modernization, and upgrading the strategic submarine missile force.

The new MX missile will enhance the survivability of our land-based intercontinental ballistic missile force. In addition, the program calls for accelerating our ability to reinforce Western Europe with massive ground and air forces.

Also, recognizing that our national interests are critically dependent on a strong and effective intelligence capability, the President is recommending we provide America's intelligence community with charters which can permit it to operate more effectively and without excessively cumbersome or self-defeating administrative requirements.

In recent years presidents of both parties have had great difficulty in getting Congress to adopt the programs they have recommended. What has caused this difficulty, and how would you go about overcoming it?

Our Founding Fathers were wise in providing for the separation of the executive, legislative, and judicial branches. The system works best for the American people. Conflicts and disagreements are inevitable, and part of the governmental process. The President believes the disagreements are often exaggerated and blown out of proportion by the media coverage. President Carter pointed out in his third annual State of the Union Message that his administration has had a very cooperative and productive record with the Congress—much more so than is generally acknowledged. Landmark legislation has been enacted. Major domestic and international problems have been addressed directly, and resolved.

In no other three-year period in our recent past has there been a comparable record of progress and achievement. The Congress is an independent branch, and its members exercise that independence as they evaluate the proposals before them.

President Carter has said that one of the pleasant surprises of his presidency has been the high level of honesty and competence and detailed knowledge by members of Congress and their staffs. He is grateful for the leadership the Congress has shown, the advice and counsel they have shared, and the partnership that has developed. The President believes this is a process which can only bring benefits to the American people.

What policies or programs will you pursue that best reflect your sense of domestic priorities for the 1980s and beyond? What sacrifices will the American people be asked to make?

As in previous years, President Carter will be working towards the achievement of several basic goals. None is easily attainable. All these objectives will require sustained dedication and, in some few cases, sacrifice. These goals are to: ensure our economic strength; create energy security for our nation; enhance basic human and social needs; make our government more efficient and effective; protect and enhance our rights and liberties; preserve and develop our natural resources; build America's military strength; and resolve international disputes through peaceful means.

These are a few of the domestic and international priorities of the President, all intended to continue America as the strongest nation on earth—militarily, economically, politically, and morally. On the domestic scene, inflation is a major challenge and the battle against inflation is linked to the national effort to restore our energy security.

President Carter believes the battle to assure America's energy independence will require some sacrifice. However, the inflation and energy programs proposed by President Carter make certain that the work and sacrifice is shared equally, with no one sector having to carry an unfair burden.

The President is extremely optimistic about the future because of his faith in the greatness and sense of decency and fairness of the American people.

Connally

JOHN B. CONNALLY was appointed secretary of the Navy in 1960 and in 1962 was elected to the first of his three terms as governor of Texas. In 1972 he became secretary of the Treasury.

Connally has also engaged in business endeavors and in the practice of law. He is now a partner in the law firm of Vinson and Elkins of Houston.

During World War II, he served in the U.S. Navy in the Pacific and in North Africa and was awarded nine battle stars. He graduated from the University of Texas law school and served as an aide to Lyndon B. Johnson in the House and Senate. Connally joined the Republican party in 1973. He was born in Floresville, Texas, in 1917.

How would you solve our nation's energy problems? Specifically, what would be the key elements of your national energy policy?

I have said throughout the past year that for the remainder of this century, we are going to have to depend on three basic sources for energy: petroleum, coal, and nuclear power. A recently completed National Academy of Sciences study confirms that finding.

We must begin immediately to mine more coal and burn more coal. Wherever feasible, we must convert utility and industrial boilers from oil and gas to coal as quickly as possible.

We should deregulate all oil and gas to encourage every possible exploration effort here at home—and this could be done today by presidential executive order.

We should simplify the federal government regulatory process to permit the construction of nuclear power plants in one-half the time presently required. At the same time, we should require more rigorous plant inspections of construction and operations to ensure maximum safeguards.

We should seek to create, along with Canada and Mexico, a North American common market for energy.

And we should continue research and development on solar, geothermal, oil shales, gasohol, fast breeder reactors, and other energy sources of long-range promise.

America has the resources and the technological knowhow to

attain energy independence. It simply must focus its will on a sensible and consistent national program to do so—immediately!

Most polls show that Americans consider inflation to be the number one domestic problem. How would you rid the economy of inflation?

There is no great mystery about inflation. When you print more money without producing more goods and services, you're going to have it.

One of the greatest contributors to inflation is excessive federal government spending. Another is the cost of imported energy. During the past decade, deficit spending has totaled a staggering $325 billion. In 1979 alone, the federal government spent about $30 billion more than it took in.

My first act as president would be an all-out effort to restrain federal spending and balance the budget. I believe this could be done within two years without reducing any essential programs. At the same time I would begin a crash program to achieve energy self-sufficiency.

I would also take aggressive steps to reduce or eliminate our foreign trade deficit, another major contributor to inflation and our eroding dollar.

Finally, I would place far more emphasis on incentives for savings and investment to modernize our nation's aging industrial base. Only if we have such modernization of our plants and equipment can we hope to compete with our more efficient competitors in world markets and achieve the increased productivity that is the ultimate answer to inflation.

The productivity growth rate of the American economy declined drastically in the 1970s. During 1979 it was negative. What steps would you take to restore productivity growth to the American economy? Do you believe we need to stimulate capital formation to aid in this? How would you do this?

For too long now, our economy has been frustrated and stagnated by federal tax policies which encourage consumption while penalizing savings and investment.

As a result, our American productive plant has become the oldest in the industrial world. Our productivity growth lags far behind that of Japan, Germany, France, Canada, and even the United Kingdom.

We're going to have to change this trend if we are to maintain a growth economy. Nothing is more critical in the change than encouragement of capital formation. And that requires a new tax philosophy.

I have advocated the stimulation of individual savings—the creation of a "taxpayer's nest egg account," of up to $10,000 with its earnings secure from federal taxation so long as it remains invested in a bank, savings and loan, or common stock. Such a plan would encourage the building of a small estate for the average wage earner and create enormous new capital for investment.

I would combine that with revision of current depreciation policies to encourage investment in new plants to achieve greater productivity. We should provide for the recovery of the cost of any building within ten years, any equipment within five years, and any rolling stock within three years.

I am convinced that these two actions would produce enormous new growth and prosperity.

Government regulation provides benefits, but it also imposes costs. What changes in the regulatory process, if any, would you propose?

First, we must focus public opinion on the enormous cost to our society and its consumers of excessive government regulation.

Estimates are that regulatory costs to business now exceed $125 billion a year, a large portion of which is borne by the consumer. The Small Business Administration recently said the cost to small business alone exceeds $12.7 billion annually.

The first step toward dealing with the problem would be the insistence that the Congress apply more workmanship in the drafting of legislation to eliminate much of the bureaucratic excess and ambiguity that now results from lack of clear intent.

Second, government agencies should be required to prepare Economic Impact Statements when contemplating new regulations. Tax policy should allow for full recovery in one year of all investments dictated by federal regulations. Regulatory programs should be subject to "sunset" mechanisms.

Finally, I have advocated that small business, which is hampered most by the cost and frustration of government regulation, be substantially exempted from provisions and paperwork requirements of federal government regulation. This final action particularly, directed at the most energetic, innovative, and creative part of our economy, would result in new vitality which would in turn produce new jobs and more taxes.

In the last several years, there has been an increased concern with environmental protection. How would you achieve a balance between the need for economic growth and protection of the environment?

Certainly most Americans share a common dedication to safeguarding our nation's environment. Nature blessed us more richly than most peoples, and ours is a magnificent treasure to protect.

I want clean air to breathe and clean water to drink, just as we all do. I am an environmentalist who has practiced his concern on his own land.

But the worst environment I can imagine is to be cold, hungry, and unemployed. And in recent years we have allowed excesses to develop—well-meaning as they may be—which could lead to such an environment if bureaucratic obsessions for total purity are allowed to strangle American industry. In some cases, the consequences of such excesses reach the point of absurdity.

We must set reasonable standards. And we must be prepared to make trade-off sacrifices—even to the point of endangering a small fish species, if necessary, to assure an adequate water supply for thousands of our citizens.

What is called for is common sense balance. We have the American ingenuity and advanced technology to utilize our resources to assure a standard of living we all want without doing undue violence to the environment.

What should the United States stand for in world affairs in the 1980s? Concretely how would you propose that American ideals and interests prevail?

I would hope that the United States in the 1980s would once again reassert its role as leader of the free world. If we fail to assume that role, who can?

To do so, we must rebuild our credibility around the globe.

We must rebuild our credibility in foreign policy with a consistency in dealing both with our allies and with our adversaries. We must rebuild our credibility in dealing with our economic problems, resolve the problems of energy and inflation and restore soundness to the dollar.

While maintaining a position of strength and insisting that our interests be respected, we should remain a beacon of hope for the rest of the world.

We should remember that, because of our system of freedom and opportunity, America has done more for more people than any other society in history. No other people have enjoyed such freedom, such security, such a highly developed standard of living. No other land has offered such a fertile climate for the fullest development of talents and genius of the individual.

In the years ahead, we shall see increased competition for the resources of the world and for the minds of men. We must be prepared to articulate the ideals and beliefs that have built this country, and have the ingenuity and the will to see that they prevail as the best possible hope for mankind in a changing world.

What would be the elements of your defense policy? How would you ensure the success of your vision of America's future in a changing and troubled world?

Unless we want to yield forever our role as leader of the free world, we must strengthen our military and intelligence capabilities. Freedom and security can be maintained only through strength.

During the past decade the Soviet Union spent about 30 percent more on defense activities than did the United States. Since 1960, the portion of our federal budget allocated to defense has dropped from 48 percent to 22 percent. We must do more.

Our strategic nuclear capabilities must be substantially strengthened through utilization of the B-1 bomber, the MX missile, and other effective systems. We should also utilize the cruise and Trident missiles.

It would be my policy to increase defense spending—not for cosmetic purposes in an election year—but sensibly and methodically over a period of years to ensure real security. It would be my policy to rebuild our intelligence agencies, recognizing the dangerous world we live in.

And I would hope that my administration would have the vision to anticipate events in a perilous world, rather than constantly reacting to crises after it is too late. Long before the current problems in Iran and Afghanistan, I called for the establishment of a military presence in the Middle East to help bring stability to that strategic area.

In recent years presidents of both parties have had great difficulty in getting Congress to adopt the programs they have recommended. What has caused this difficulty, and how would you go about overcoming it?

The problems described may be attributed in large degree to shortcomings in communications, both on a one-to-one basis and to the public in general.

The president's powers to influence events rest primarily on his effectiveness in dealing with individual members of Congress and in mobilizing the support of the American people for his programs. Lack of experience in the former and an inconsistency and failure to inspire in the latter have contributed largely to the current administration's problems.

Having had personal experience with the leaders in Congress of both parties for more than forty years, some of it as a cabinet officer, I believe I know how to deal effectively with lawmakers on the Hill in an atmosphere of mutual respect.

Just as important, I believe I can articulate to the American people the problems we face and the actions necessary to deal with those problems in the 1980s. I have great faith in the people of this country, once convinced of the course we should follow, to rally behind its leader.

I have equal confidence that the Congress, if perceiving a united country, will respond positively to enlightened leadership.

What policies or programs will you pursue that best reflect your sense of domestic priorities for the 1980s and beyond? What sacrifices will the American people be asked to make?

Without question, our top domestic priorities for the years just ahead should be energy and inflation.

Unless and until we rectify our current level of dependence on oil imports, we remain hostages to the OPEC nations with peril to our very security. I would therefore pursue a policy of utmost urgency to move toward energy independence for America, an action affecting the life of every citizen.

Inflation is equally devastating and pervasive in its impact on American lives and even more insidious. I would immediately institute policies to deal with it as vigorously as possible.

I would place high priority on careful scrutiny of the structure and efficiency of the entire federal bureaucracy and its impact on our citizens. The current delivery systems of our social programs should be reexamined and revamped. We need to make sure that the bureaucracy does not consume too much of the resources of the programs, and that the benefits reach the intended beneficiaries.

We need to place a priority on the strengthening and better financing of our vital social security program.

Obviously, these and other domestic priorities can be addressed only in an atmosphere of national security and tranquility. Therefore, the strength of our defense capabilities must always share priority.

Crane

PHILIP M. CRANE has been a member of the U.S. House of Representatives from Illinois since 1969. A ranking Republican on the House Ways and Means Committee, he serves on the Public Assistance and Unemployment Compensation and the Health subcommittees. He founded the Republican Study Committee.

Crane served with the U.S. Army in Europe in 1955–1956. He studied at Hillsdale College, the University of Michigan, and the University of Vienna, and received an M.A. and Ph.D. from Indiana University. After teaching at Indiana University and Bradley University, he became director of schools of Westminster Academy in Northbrook, Illinois. He is the author of *The Democrat's Dilemma; The Sum of Good Government;* and *Surrender in Panama.* He was born in 1930 in Chicago, Ill.

How would you solve our nation's energy problems? Specifically, what would be the key elements of your national energy policy?

We need to realize that there really is no energy shortage from natural causes, but rather a misallocation of energy resulting from years of government intervention in the marketplace. If we expect our economy to grow, we will need energy for new plants and businesses. Therefore, we have two options: increase domestic energy supplies or increase imports. It is ludicrous to insinuate either that we can "save our way out" of this energy shortage or that we should increase our reliance on foreign sources that already gravely jeopardize our national security. The only way to remedy this government-created crisis is to encourage domestic production by getting government out of the energy business and allowing the market to sort out the cheapest and most efficient energy alternatives. We can become energy self-sufficient by: decontrolling prices; putting our expert private producers back in control of energy production; cutting regulations policed by a massive bureaucracy; streamlining the licensing process for all power plants, especially nuclear plants; opening potentially energy-rich public lands; shifting import emphasis away from unfriendly or unstable nations to neighboring friends; getting tougher with OPEC

40

through our international market power; and appointing an energy secretary who is effective in dealing with the Congress and American allies abroad, who would share my commitment to increase energy production and economic growth, and who understands the workings of our free market until Congress can be persuaded to abolish the Department of Energy.

America cannot continue to grow without energy production. Consequently, our federal energy policy should be to enhance the production of gas and oil, both at home and in friendly neighboring nations. The largest recoverable coal reserves lie within our borders, and this must be mined, burned, and converted. Nuclear power will make the biggest contribution in meeting our near- and long-term energy needs. Nuclear technology and the fast breeder reactor must continue to be developed. We must develop a policy that allows us to utilize our great natural resources and lets the American economic system function without restraint.

Most polls show that Americans consider inflation to be the number one domestic problem. How would you rid the economy of inflation?

Before discussing inflation remedies, it is essential to define our terms. Inflation is an expansion of the money supply in excess of productivity increases. Neither business nor labor causes inflation, though they are often blamed by those who advocate restricting their wages and prices. The federal government causes inflation. The Federal Reserve System resorts to money expansion to finance the monstrous deficits created by Congress. This practice is called "monetization" of debt in Washington. In the rest of the country it is called counterfeiting, and it has the same effect. It makes the money worth less; that results in higher prices; that causes labor to seek higher wages; and that compounds the price spiral problem. Business and labor, however, are not causing the problem; they are only responding to the government-created problem.

To solve the problem, we must amend the Constitution to restrain federal spending. My proposal, introduced in Congress long before the concept took root nationwide, would forbid any federal spending in excess of 33⅓ percent of the average national income. The federal budget has grown 400 percent over the last fifteen years. Unless we place a constitutional check on the growth of government spending, it will continue to inflate the currency and injure pensioners, wage earners, and savers.

Studies indicate that such an amendment linking growth in federal spending to growth in personal and national income would produce budget surpluses in two years. Any surpluses should be rebated in tax cuts and used to retire the national debt.

The productivity growth rate of the American economy declined drastically in the 1970s. During 1979 it was negative. What steps would you take to restore productivity growth to the American economy? Do you believe we need to stimulate capital formation to aid in this? How would you do this?

High taxes are crippling our economy. By taking a big slice of any economic gain, the government is reducing the incentive and resources for continual growth. We desperately need a permanent, across-the-board bracket reduction of at least 30 percent to restore the reward for working, saving, producing, investing, and growing, as my good friend and colleague Jack Kemp has proposed. This would result in a 33 percent tax cut after three years if one is in a $40,000 per year tax bracket, but the tax cut percentage increases as one goes down the economic ladder. Thus, a taxpayer earning $8,000 per year would have his taxes reduced 90 percent.

This is, however, only a beginning. Savings in this nation are the lowest in any major industrial nation: only 3.3 percent of disposable income in 1979. By comparison, the Japanese saved approximately 25 percent, the Germans 15 percent, and the French 13 percent. No wonder interest rates are astronomical. With the government borrowing to cover its deficits and discouraging private savings with inflation and taxes, the lending institutions have a limited supply of money on hand. Its price has to be high. Eliminating all taxation on savings would help to restore the encouragement to save.

To raise a paltry $6 billion (less that 1 percent of what it spends), the government also imposes inheritance taxes. This is, by definition, a tax on widows and orphans. Although designed to break up concentrations of wealth, these taxes only seem to break up small businesses and farms which may be about to prosper despite enormous tax burdens when their owner commits his last dignified taxable act: he dies. Estate and gift taxes should be entirely eliminated.

In addition, we must increase the investment tax credit to 15 percent, accelerate depreciation allowances on capital investments, abolish double taxation of dividends, and index the tax code. Until we restore the reward for capital formation, businesses will not have the resources to expand and hire new employees. With the tax changes I have suggested, America can become again the world's most productive nation.

Government regulation provides benefits, but it also imposes costs. What changes in the regulatory process, if any, would you propose?

Recent studies have concluded that federal regulations are now costing consumers over $100 billion a year or more—an amount roughly equal to one-half of all federal income taxes paid each year in this country. Every taxpayer, then, is paying an indirect tax equal to one-half his yearly income tax to support federally imposed regulations. The result is a reduced standard of living in America. Prices of things people demand continually rise as manufacturers must pass along the increased cost mandated by regulations in order to stay in business. Ordinary people can afford less and less; their living style declines. Unless we reverse the trend—the *Federal Register* of regulations has grown from 21,900 pages a year when President Carter was elected in 1976 to 35,000 pages in 1979—the downward spiral will continue.

Economic impact statements and cost-benefit analyses should precede all regulations. If these exceed congressional guidelines, no regulation should go into effect without the affirmative action of Congress. In addition, I advocate "sunset legislation" that sets a time limit on the life of any regulatory agency. At a fixed time, the agency is disbanded unless it can prove to Congress that it should continue in business. Congress, in turn, would have to openly vote to preserve the agency, which would at least help fix the responsibility for the conflicting, confusing, and costly regulatory climate we all endure. Finally, whenever the government sues a citizen to enforce its regulations and fails, the government should reimburse the successful defendant for the legal fees consumed in defeating its suit.

In the last several years, there has been an increased concern with environmental protection. How would you achieve a balance between the need for economic growth and protection of the environment?

Everyone wants a clean and healthy environment. Everyone also wants a job, a decent income, and lower prices. In recent years I have visited many areas of our land where those values come into conflict. In Youngstown, Ohio, where I met with some top union officials, the steel mill was closed down and thousands put out of work in the wake of costly demands by the Environmental Protection Agency. Too often in recent years, the government has chosen to enforce environmentalism where it has been clear that large numbers of jobs were endangered. On some occasions, federal agencies have stretched existing laws to the extreme with apparent indifference to the serious economic harm they have caused ordinary people.

We must return more environmental decisions to the state and local level where the trade-offs are known and the impacts will be directly experienced. Community consensus should be respected. Why should a few people representing a federal agency in Washington be able to make decisions that fundamentally change the lives of thousands in Cheyenne, Wyoming, or Des Moines, Iowa, or Youngstown, Ohio? Until the process of moving the decision-making process to the states is complete, no regulations should be approved without a clear showing of compelling health benefits that totally override economic considerations.

What should the United States stand for in world affairs in the 1980s? Concretely how would you propose that American ideals and interests prevail?

For the past four years American foreign policy has been a failure, a disgrace. American prestige, American credibility, American influence has declined continuously and precipitously. Since President Carter assumed office we have failed to offer strong and effective response to the Soviet-armed Cuban Afrika Korps adventures in Angola and Ethiopia. We abandoned longtime friends and allies in Iran and Nicaragua while allowing admittedly destabilizing forces to prevail. We were irresolute in the face of the introduction of Soviet combat troops, advanced nuclear-capable fighter-bombers and improved submarine servicing facilities in Cuba. Is it any wonder that our friends perceive us as weak, that they doubt our willingness to confront a Soviet challenge, whether direct or through surrogates, wherever it may occur? We cannot expect other pro-Western, free nations to support our ideals and consider them precious if we are unwilling to stand up for them. We cannot foster and champion the spread of basic human freedoms and counter Soviet aggression if we sit idly by and watch Americans taken hostage and sovereign nations overrun by Soviet tanks.

The time has come for us to act. We must develop a cohesive, comprehensive foreign policy and pursue it actively. We must spend whatever is necessary to regain military superiority. We must assure our friends and allies that we are willing to stand firmly behind our principles.

We must reestablish a reputation for standing behind our commitments and friends. Our idealistic support for human rights is the foundation of our foreign policy, but that commitment must be tempered with the realistic awareness that the world is as it is, not as it ought to be, and that we cannot make it over in our own image. We should be mindful of Ben Franklin's admonition—"A good example is the best sermon."

What would be the elements of your defense policy? How would you ensure the success of your vision of America's future in a changing and troubled world?

The United States must be militarily superior. The nature of geo-political competition with the Soviet Union demands it. Their policy is to take advantage of, and exploit, any opportunity offered. If we are equal to them militarily—have parity or essential equivalence— we are not going to be in a position to advance our ideals as a positive influence. A free democratic society that tolerates parity with a centralized totalitarian system is going to be constantly on the defensive. We need to be able to enter any confrontation (and there will be some) with as few strikes against us as possible.

True peace is only attainable through strength. America is currently perceived as being in a weakened state. The President has created this perception by remaining excessively preoccupied with obtaining peace through unilateral concessions. If we are to avoid that trap, we need to take steps now to restore our strategic and conventional force structures to meet the Soviet challenges in the 1980s and 1990s.

President Carter has eroded our position vis-à-vis the Soviets with drastic cuts in defense spending. He cut $5 billion from the last Ford defense budget. He slashed $57 billion from Ford's five-year defense program proposal. He cancelled the B-1 bomber. He vetoed funding for the nuclear aircraft carrier. He shelved development and deployment of the neutron weapon. He delayed the cruise missile, Trident missile and submarine, and MX ICBM programs. He closed the Minuteman III ICBM production line. These cuts have fed the global perception that the United States is but a shadow of its former self.

To regain superiority we must revitalize our defense and intelligence programs. That means increased funding. We must allocate more defense funding for research and development, an area we have traditionally excelled in but have allowed to slip considerably. We must craft our defense posture to deal with Soviet capabilities, not speculation as to their intentions. We must regain superiority in strategic weapons. Unless we build a strong mix of strategic defenses, we will never be able to survive a nuclear attack and win the resultant war. If the Soviets believe they can win a nuclear war, they may be tempted in a crisis to try. We must strengthen our military capabilities.

45

We need to ensure that our active forces are up to combat levels of manning, equipment, weapons, and ammunition of the qualities necessary to meet the needs of the 1980s. The same approach must be earnestly and vigorously applied to the reserves and National Guard. All this will require an increased defense budget.

The best military force in the world is of limited value if it is not at or cannot get to a crisis in a timely fashion. The United States must undertake a military strategy which positions our forces in or near areas of instability and provides the capability for rapid reinforcement. The Middle East—especially the Persian Gulf, the southwest Asia region, the littoral area of the Arabian Sea—is such an area. To protect our interests and stabilize the area, American military presence is needed. A new fleet, with ports, air fields, communication and logistical support facilities. We must have arrangements for use of air space, air fields, and bases to receive and redeploy U.S. troops. Further, we must improve our relations with the regional nations and consider alliances.

Finally, any military presence and capabilities we develop must be coupled with an active, coherent foreign policy aimed at discouraging and denying Soviet adventurism in the region involved.

In recent years presidents of both parties have had great difficulty in getting Congress to adopt the programs they have recommended. What has caused this difficulty, and how would you go about overcoming it?

Presidents in the recent past have had trouble convincing Congress to adopt their policies for several reasons. Some factors contributing to their difficulty can be isolated: imperial presidencies, divisive policies, trust and integrity, competence and knowledgeability, and education and articulation.

First, the imperial presidency. We all remember the sarcasm directed by members and press toward the White House during the Nixon era. We have never as a people taken well to the pretensions of monarchy and have found delight in humbling the mighty. Many have forgotten that the halcyon days of JFK's Camelot resulted in the White House and Congress being at loggerheads.

Next, divisive policies. National policies must be in harmony with basic American values to produce a national consensus that can be translated into congressional policy. American values do not permit us to wage political, no-win wars. The consensus in the Gulf of Tonkin resolution in 1964 was bound to deteriorate once Americans concluded that their boys were being sent into war without a speedy military victory as the objective.

Trust and integrity. Americans still tend to revere the institution of the presidency as the face our nation presents to the world. We believe, not inappropriately, that our values and ideals are superior to all others. Any public revelations that tarnish that national image erode the climate of national support necessary to win the support of Congress.

Competence and knowledgeability. Congress, perhaps more than even the American people, respects evidence of an administration that understands the nature of the congressional system, the protocols and properties preserved through almost two centuries of tradition. Congress for all of its changes is still an institution filled with traditions that are preserved and respected. Any president who neither understands nor respects the committee system, seniority prerogatives, and leadership power is a president destined to have trouble with Congress.

Finally, education and articulation. The President must have a keen understanding of problems that can be presented effectively to voters to create public sentiment. The goal is to engineer a climate of opinion that will make it "good politics" for members of Congress to do the right thing even if they are doing it for the wrong reason.

What policies or programs will you pursue that best reflect your sense of domestic priorities for the 1980s and beyond? What sacrifices will the American people be asked to make?

This nation was founded upon a profound respect for individual freedom. Our Constitution was drafted to protect the individual's right to pursue happiness in his own way without interference from the government or individuals who may wish to impose their wills on others. We have fought wars to protect that freedom.

Yet in our day, this reverence for the worth of individuals and their right to choose for themselves is threatened by the growth of government. Every day government bureaucrats dream up new ways to regulate and tax us. Strand by strand, these elitist regulators and taxers are fashioning a rope strong enough to bind even the strong-willed American people. This is not what the Founding Fathers had in mind. Government was to defend freedom, not abridge it. We need to catch a vision of what the Constitution was creating for us and our children. We need to halt the growth of government and taxes. We need to strengthen our defenses against foreign nations intent upon seeing our system crumble. We need to return the individual to his place of prominence.

To accomplish this, we need to pursue several specific programs. We need:

- a constitutional amendment to restrain federal spending which would achieve a balanced budget and control inflation
- an across-the-board tax bracket reduction of at least 30 percent as proposed by my good friend and colleague Jack Kemp
- an end to taxation on all interest earned on savings accounts
- an end to all estate and gift taxes
- an end to double taxation on dividends
- an annual adjustment in tax brackets to prevent inflation from forcing taxpayers to pay more in taxes, known as tax indexing
- an increase in the investment tax credit to 15 percent
- an acceleration in depreciation allowances
- a reduction in corporate taxes
- a cost-benefit analysis to curb regulations harmful to American jobs
- a restoration of the predominant role of state and community governments in environmental, moral, welfare, and other decisions
- an overall strengthening of our defense capability

These are just a few suggested improvements to return government to its proper role as servant, rather than master; as defender, rather than usurper, of freedom.

Dole

ROBERT J. DOLE has been a Republican member of the U.S. Senate from Kansas since 1968. He serves on the Senate Judiciary and Agriculture committees and is the ranking Republican on the Finance Committee. In 1976 he became the Republican candidate for vice-president of the United States.

While serving with the U.S. Army in Italy in World War II, Dole was wounded twice and decorated twice for heroic achievement. He attended the University of Kansas and graduated from Washburn University law school. After being elected to the Kansas Legislature, Dole served four terms as Russell County attorney and four terms in the U.S. House of Representatives. He was born in Russell, Kansas, in 1923.

How would you solve our nation's energy problems? Specifically, what would be the key elements of your national energy policy?

It has been approximately three years since President Carter declared the energy crisis to be the moral equivalent of war. Yet, America today faces more serious energy problems than it did three years ago. We have continued to become more and more dependent on oil from unstable foreign sources. We have continued to send a greater share of our gross national product abroad to pay the tribute that the OPEC cartel extracts. Now we face the threat of increasing Soviet influence over the Persian Gulf, which produces 25 percent of the world's oil.

What can we do to solve this problem?

First, we must unleash American industry's ability to produce more energy. For example, we should open more offshore and onshore federal lands for oil and gas exploration, with the appropriate environmental safeguards. Also, the decontrol of crude oil prices will do much to stimulate increased domestic oil exploration. Industry experts have estimated that decontrol will result in a 4-million-barrel-per-day increase in production by the mid to late 1980s. Unfortunately the so-called windfall profits tax will substantially undercut the expected production benefits of decontrol.

Second, as part of a coordinated expansion of energy production, we need to encourage greater utilization of alternatives to oil and natural gas. These alternatives include coal, which can be gasified and liquefied; oil shale; gasohol, wood and other biomass products; hydroelectric power; solar, wind, and geothermal power. We also need to make an intensified effort to develop adequate safety and spent fuel disposal procedures for nuclear facilities so that we can continue and expand our own use of nuclear power.

Finally, we must take steps to use energy more efficiently. Energy experts almost universally agree that an effective energy conservation program will be the fastest, cleanest, and most cost effective means of expanding our domestic energy supply. Experiments have demonstrated that as much as two-thirds of residential heating energy can be saved by the proper conservation steps, with no loss in comfort. Consequently, we must encourage such residential and industrial conservation through tax incentives, regulatory action, and other appropriate government action.

Most polls show that Americans consider inflation to be the number one domestic problem. How would you rid the economy of inflation?

There is no simple solution to the serious inflation problem that this country is facing. Years of reckless spending, an often incorrect monetary policy, increasing unproductive expenditures on federal regulation, and a lack of a responsible energy policy have created this economic problem.

There are, however, several specific steps that will both slow inflation to tolerable levels and that will prevent its recurrence in our society.

First, fiscal policy—the government's taxing and spending policy —must be basically altered. Excessive government spending contributes fundamentally to inflation by pumping more money into the economy without correspondingly increasing production. We must cut spending now and pass a constitutional amendment that limits spending and taxing and requires a balanced federal budget.

Secondly, tax policy in this country has tended more and more in recent years to discourage needed capital formation and to encourage consumption. A healthy private sector requires a large capital stock to increase its productivity and its international competitiveness. Tax policy must be radically restructured to this end.

The nation's monetary policy—essentially the control of the economy's supply of money and credit—is also an important element in fighting inflation. By cutting budget deficits, the Congress can decrease the pressure on the Federal Reserve Board to expand the money supply. Further, through their oversight functions, the president and the Congress can encourage sound monetary policy.

Thirdly, the Congress should act to eliminate much of the current, unnecessary federal regulations. The country must be made aware of the huge costs which the economy pays for this activity, and every federal regulation should be reviewed to determine if it is worth its cost. Those which do not measure up must be eliminated.

Numerous other important steps must also be taken. For example, this country must develop a rational energy policy. We cannot continue to ship billions of dollars overseas to purchase oil while discouraging domestic energy production.

The productivity growth rate of the American economy declined drastically in the 1970s. During 1979 it was negative. What steps would you take to restore productivity growth to the American economy? Do you believe we need to stimulate capital formation to aid in this? How would you do this?

I believe that a strong, growing economy is essential to a free nation. It assures a constantly higher standard of living and upward social mobility for all its citizens. No free economy can consistently grow or long remain strong if business does not have access to sufficient capital for improvement in efficiency and expansion. A country with a tax system that encourages consumption and discourages investment, savings, and capital formation is engaged in a policy that will eventually threaten the essence of its freedom.

Unfortunately, the United States has for too long been on such a course. Among major industrialized nations, our country ranks last in savings as a percent of income, last in fixed investment as a percent of GNP, and last in productivity growth. Is it any wonder that we have uncovered the secret of prolonged high levels of inflation even during times of low economic growth?

The only solution to this problem is also no secret. We must radically restructure our tax system. Some small but important steps have been taken in recent months. Congress reduced the capital gains tax rates last year, and this past December the Senate added a savings interest and dividend exclusion amendment to the energy tax bill.

Much, much more remains to be done, however. We must reduce the regular rates on all sources of individual and corporate income as well as further reduce the capital gains rate; outdated historical cost depreciation methods must be replaced with a simpler, more accelerated method; the double taxation of corporate profits and dividends must be reduced; and special tax credits for research and development must be enacted.

51

Our current dilemma cannot be reversed overnight, but the prescription is clear, and the first major steps are long overdue.

Government regulation provides benefits, but it also imposes costs. What changes in the regulatory process, if any, would you propose?

Whether articulated as unnecessary, inefficient, or overly burdensome and costly regulation, increasingly angry criticism has been directed at federal regulation. Leaving the decade in which the regulatory landscape as we know it was created, we must ask whether the benefits of the unprecedented regulatory activity of the 1970s were worth the resulting drain on the productive energies of our economy.

The unvarnished answer is that we have asked our government to protect us from an expanding category of risks, whether on our roads, in our factories, in business competition, or in our natural environment. This effort has been made only at an extreme price borne by the consumer, estimated to reach over $100 billion this year, which aggravates our already high rate of inflation.

Experience shows that the free market remains relatively the most efficient and humane economic "regulator," indicating further deregulation to be the sound policy course. To improve necessary regulation, I have proposed legislation, the Rulemaking Improvements Act, which would reintroduce market common sense into the regulatory process by subjecting proposed regulations to a form of cost-benefit analysis. Finally, we must adopt other, nonregulatory approaches, such as effluent taxes to discourage pollution, which, by maintaining free choice in the market, preserve the vitality of our economy.

In the last several years, there has been an increased concern with environmental protection. How would you achieve a balance between the need for economic growth and protection of the environment?

Environmental protection and energy independence. Realizing both will be one of our greatest challenges in the 1980s. As conventional energy sources deplete, there will be an inevitable call to ease federal restrictions on clean air, clean water, and natural preservation.

I believe we must preserve our environment while at the same time expanding production of domestic energy supplies. The land, seas, and atmosphere can be preserved under the Clean Air Act, the Clean Water Act, the Endangered Species Act, and the Endangered Wildlife Act—all necessary environmental laws which I support.

But, too, we must be prepared to extract all available domestic energy supplies from both land and sea, lest the energy crisis become an economic and energy disaster for the American people. To this end, I believe we must greatly increase our utilization of coal, agriculture based fuels, and domestic petroleum. Energy producers should be encouraged, not discouraged, to fully develop—within reasonable environmental standards—the energy reserves we possess. We simply cannot continue to overregulate energy producers by enforcing standards that are unreasonable or unreachable. We must balance the often-competing interests of energy and the environment, and I believe this balance can be met.

It is my intention to call for an overall review of our federal air and water regulations in our drive for energy self-sufficiency. I do not believe it will be necessary to substantially alter our environmental policies, but when excessive government regulations can be reduced it is our duty to act. We must expedite development of solar, wind, and geothermal power and other so-called clean sources of energy, including gasohol, one of the most feasible short-term solutions. Minor variances from environmental standards may be necessary in order to achieve our goal of energy self-sufficiency. However, we cannot turn our back on our longstanding commitment to the preservation of our most important national resource—the environment.

What should the United States stand for in world affairs in the 1980s? Concretely how would you propose that American ideals and interests prevail?

One of my major concerns for quite some time has been the status of the United States in world politics and the lack of a coherent approach to foreign policy. The apparent infirmness on the part of the Carter administration toward various crises has been obvious over the past few years. As a result, the United States has appeared weak to its allies and without the will to protect its vital interests. Such weaknesses cannot go unchecked without irreparable damage to our nation and its people. Therefore, I feel the first priority for American leadership in the new decade should be a reassessment of our national strategic goals—the determination of what our foreign policy should be and how our relations with the other superpower, the Soviet Union, should change. We ought to repair our alliance systems with our allies and urge closer relations between the nonaligned states and ourselves. It is imperative that we develop a strong foreign policy so that other countries are assured they can depend upon our assistance, and so that we are able to address events around the world with decisive, strong, and effective action in keeping with our foreign policy objectives and our nation's national interest. The crisis in Iran and the shock over the seizure of American hostages has demonstrated that the American people are ready and willing to rally behind our President, to present a united and solid front to our allies and to the rest of the world. But this support must have behind it strong and effective measures taken by the administration over the long term, to address such situations, and to prepare our capabilities to meet them.

This is especially imperative now in order to effectively check the ever-growing Soviet aggression and expansion we are witnessing in many vital regions of the globe. The Soviet Union has beefed up their Pacific fleet and now use the Camrahn Bay Navy Base we built in Vietnam. Their Mediterranean and Indian Ocean fleets have grown dangerously. There is a continuing buildup of Soviet naval strength in Cuba, which parallels the introduction of a Russian combat brigade on Cuban soil, which the President apparently was forced to accept last summer. Moscow's latest threat is the invasion of Afghanistan, with the ultimate goal of regional destabilization and eventual control of the vast oil reserves in the Middle East. This most recent development is a blatant example of Soviet aggression. It should finally lay to rest the misperceptions in this country, Europe, and particularly the Third World of Moscow's intentions on the world scene, for Soviet policy represents a dangerous challenge to world peace. Russian imperialism was never more apparent than in this unprovoked invasion of a friendly nation, and I feel it will have a profound impact on the alignment of all the Third World countries—but only if we have a policy ready to take advantage of the opportunity, and the strength and commitment to make the policy credible.

What would be the elements of your defense policy? How would you ensure the success of your vision of America's future in a changing and troubled world?

It is essential that we develop a strong and effective foreign policy, and that we also achieve and maintain a strong military capability to back up our foreign policy decisions and actions. The record clearly shows that Russia has conducted one of the most massive arms build-ups in history during the negotiations for a SALT II. In contrast, our defense policy has been characterized by cancellations and cutbacks of systems and forces critical to America's future security and stability.

When Mr. Carter was running for president in 1976, he claimed he would trim from $7 billion to $15 billion from our defense budget. Unfortunately, he succeeded. During that time and to this day, I have warned that these defense cuts could lead us into a risk of war. Now we are faced with the possibility of reinstating the draft and a crash program to beef up an all-too-lean defense budget. Perhaps our weakest area after the Vietnam War was in the number of navy ships available for our conventional, as well as strategic, commitment. Carter cut the projected navy budget through 1983 by almost $26 billion. In addition, in his first two years in office, he slashed our navy ship-building plan to replace our aging fleet with 157 new ships by 1982, by over half. In the strategic sector, in order to buy SALT II, the Carter administration delayed or cancelled vital programs. The MX missile, designed to prevent Russia from achieving a first-strike capability, will be delayed at least four years until 1989, at a time when our Minuteman missiles will become increasingly vulnerable to Soviet strategic strength. Further, in 1977, Carter cancelled the B-1 bomber program, which would have brought 244 modern aircraft on line to replace the aging B-52s. The Trident submarine procurement under Mr. Carter was cut back, and the initial operational deployment was delayed by two years. The neutron bomb, a valuable weapon for securing the NATO flank, was cancelled. It is no wonder that our strategic capability has been seriously questioned, by both our potential allies and our very real enemies.

It is essential and vital to our nation's security and the security of our allies that we fill the existing gap in our defense budget, caused by previous, unwise cutbacks and the effects of the excessive rate of inflation during past Carter years. We cannot allow ourselves to be put in a vulnerable or compromising position in world affairs. I believe a strong, coherent, and decisive foreign policy, coupled with an equally strong and effective military capability, must be our major emphasis in the 1980s, to ensure that American ideals and interests prevail, and to restore the United States to its preeminent world power role. We have seen that the American people will stand behind our President, presenting a united and strong front, which is vital and necessary. In order to bring this about, the President must begin to show a clearer understanding of world events and develop a more comprehensive and decisive foreign policy. The 1980 State of the Union speech marked a change in tone, but was unfortunately short on specifics. Now he and the Congress must begin to turn his strong rhetoric into concrete and effective action.

In recent years presidents of both parties have had great difficulty in getting Congress to adopt the programs they have recommended. What has caused this difficulty, and how would you go about overcoming it?

The basis for the apparent conflict between the executive and the Congress is often founded in a simple failure to communicate in the same terms on a given problem. Rightly or wrongly, the federal government has become increasingly complex and with that complexity has come an army of intermediaries between the Congress and the president. This diffusion or dilution, if you will, of direct contact brings with it the potential for misunderstanding. It is here, rather than in ideology or political priorities, that much of the problem lies.

Despite his many burdens, the president must put his legislative program into a higher category of priority and carve out more time for direct contact with the Congress. Liaison, however well-performed and well-intentioned, cannot be a substitute for personal effort on both sides of the aisle. The more the president is a stranger to the Congress, the less effective will he be in shepherding his legislative programs through an increasingly fractious Congress.

Without regard to whether or not one supported the specific programs involved, President Ford's term in office is a textbook example of an executive using the powers and influence of his office to accomplish his legislative goals. President Ford was an alumnus of the Congress before assuming the presidency, unlike President Carter, who had had no previous Washington experience. I think this contrast illustrates a basic fact, namely, that in order for a president to be effective in his relations with Congress, he needs to have first-hand knowledge of Capitol Hill himself. We have seen over the past three and one-half years a White House continually sending conflicting signals to the Congress and unable to communicate with and persuade congressmen and senators on legislation. I have been a member of Congress for twenty years, serving in both the House and Senate. I know the system and how it operates.

Although the question begs a complex solution the answer is really quite simple. In order to make Washington work and be responsive to the people it serves, those in charge need to know how Washington works.

What policies or programs will you pursue that best reflect your sense of domestic priorities for the 1980s and beyond? What sacrifices will the American people be asked to make?

The most important domestic problem—indeed the root of most of our domestic problems—is inflation. It is inflation that threatens the standard of living of our citizens. It is inflation that increases our taxes. And it is inflation that lowers real economic growth, thus robbing our poor of the hope of upward social mobility.

A new administration must make its highest priority reducing the current inflation to tolerable levels and preventing its recurrence in our society. A number of specific steps can be taken to this end.

First, fiscal policy—the government's taxing and spending policy —must be basically altered. Excessive government spending contributes fundamentally to inflation by pumping more money into the economy without correspondingly increasing production. We must cut spending now and pass a constitutional amendment that limits spending and taxing and requires a balanced federal budget.

Secondly, tax policy in this country has tended more and more in recent years to discourage needed capital formation and to encourage consumption. A healthy private sector requires a large capital stock to increase its productivity and its international competitiveness. Tax policy must be radically restructured to this end.

Thirdly, the nation's monetary policy—essentially the control of the economy's supply of money and credit—must be controlled to allow steady growth.

Fourthly, the Congress should act to eliminate much of the current, unnecessary federal regulation.

Numerous other important steps must also be taken. For example, this country must develop a rational energy policy. We cannot continue to ship billions of dollars overseas to purchase oil while discouraging domestic energy production.

Kennedy

EDWARD MOORE KENNEDY has been a U.S. senator from Massachusetts since 1962. In that year he was elected on the Democratic ticket to fill the unexpired term of his brother, President John F. Kennedy.

Senator Kennedy is chairman of the Senate Committee on the Judiciary, the Health and Scientific Research Subcommittee of the Senate Committee on Labor and Human Resources, and the Energy Subcommittee of the Joint Economic Committee. He has also served as chairman of the Technology Assessment Board. His publications include *In Critical Condition: The Crisis in America's Health Care* and *Decisions for a Decade.*

A 1954 graduate of Harvard University, he attended the International Law School in The Hague, Holland, and the University of Virginia Law School, where he received his LL.B. in 1959. He was born in Boston in 1932.

How would you solve our nation's energy problems? Specifically, what would be the key elements of your national energy policy?

I believe the key elements of an effective national energy policy must be:

- the immediate implementation of gasoline rationing, coupled with mass transit employer-based commuter programs and preferential treatment of van pools and car pools, to break our dangerous oil dependence on the Persian Gulf
- a sustained, aggressive program of positive incentives—grants, loans, and rebates—to reward and encourage homeowners, businessmen, and industries for investing in energy efficiency measures, like insulation, computerized energy management systems, and heat recuperators
- rapid commercialization of renewable energy technologies of all forms—especially passive and active solar space and water heaters, hydroelectricity from existing small dams, steam electricity, heat from biomass and solid waste, as well as use of wind and gasohol
- conversion of oil-burning utilities to clean-burning coal
- a limited synthetic fuel program to test the commercial, technological, and environmental feasibility of a variety of synfuels

• a moratorium on new nuclear power plants pending the implementation of recommendations from studies by the Kemeny Commission, the Nuclear Regulatory Commission, and congressional and industry task forces on the accident at Three Mile Island

• imposition of crude and product controls to protect against the sudden inflationary shocks of 100 percent OPEC price hikes and corporate windfall profits.

We must cure our addiction to foreign oil. Unless we put our energy house in order, our strength and credibility will continue to fall and the world will grow steadily more dangerous for our country and our interests.

Most polls show that Americans consider inflation to be the number one domestic problem. How would you rid the economy of inflation?

The Carter administration has failed utterly to control inflation, with last year's rate of 13.2 percent the worst since 1946. Its short-run antiinflationary efforts have been inadequate and unfair, and its long-run answers have been nonexistent. The underlying structural economic problems must be addressed, beginning immediately.

First, I would urge carefully targeted tax incentives and patent reform to encourage innovation and retooling of our industries in order to promote greater productivity.

Second, I would encourage competition by removing burdensome regulation where competition would thereby be enhanced and by focusing antitrust enforcement on the largest concentrated sectors of the economy.

Third, I would make American firms more competitive abroad by unifying America's governmental policies and offices relating to trade and by improving the financial and technical assistance terms American firms can offer when they seek to sell abroad.

Finally, I would undertake a comprehensive energy policy aimed at reducing our dependence on foreign oil through direct conservation investments in industry, business, and residences, supporting coal production and utility conversion to coal, and developing appropriate other alternative forms.

The above steps are aimed at the long-term underlying problems. In the short term, to break the back of the inflation psychology, I have proposed a six-month freeze on wages, prices, interests, rents, and profit, followed by fair mandatory controls for a limited additional period. Similarly, to reduce our dependence on OPEC I have proposed short-term gasoline rationing to reduce imports over three years in an amount equal to the 1.7 million barrels per day we now import from the Persian Gulf. These latter actions are the unpleasant last resorts forced on us by the mismanagement of economic and energy policies by the Carter administration, which has now become irretrievable.

The productivity growth rate of the American economy declined drastically in the 1970s. During 1979 it was negative. What steps would you take to restore productivity growth to the American economy? Do you believe we need to stimulate capital formation to aid in this? How would you do this?

A top priority on our economic agenda must be a major new national commitment to the twin goals of productivity and innovation. That means new incentives for savings and investment, for entrepreneurs and business firms. I see five major initiatives that can be used to reach these goals.

• First, we must provide additional incentives to encourage capital formation and to enable industries to bring their plants and equipment into the modern world. It is time to revise the tax treatment of depreciation to ensure that it is better designed to meet the four important goals of capital formation, efficiency, equity, and simplicity.

• Second, we must devise targeted incentives to stimulate ventures that hold the promise of substantial innovation.

• Third, we must revamp the antiquated patent system, so that competitive forces can play a greater role in generating innovation in the economy.

• Fourth, we must provide small business firms with new incentives to stimulate innovation. In recent decades, small business has accounted for nearly half of all major U.S. innovation.

• Fifth, we must revitalize the foundation for new technology by strengthening the nation's basic and applied research and by bolstering education and career development for scientists and engineers.

Government regulation provides benefits, but it also imposes costs. What changes in the regulatory process, if any, would you propose?

For the past six years, I have been in the forefront of efforts to eliminate the costs and burdens of excessive government regulation which have frustrated a growing number of American consumers and businesses.

We can all agree that some of the costs created by regulation are necessary to deal with many of the complex social and economic problems which we face in a modern, technological society. But in other areas, excessive regulation has stifled competition, entrenched giant firms, hurt productivity, and caused higher prices for consumers and businesses alike.

In a time of double-digit inflation and scarce energy resources, we cannot tolerate the costs created by unnecessary government interference in the marketplace.

I believe that the best approach to accomplishing meaningful regulatory reform is to take a fresh look at our regulatory process —agency-by-agency, program-by-program—with a presumption that regulation should be used only where the market does not work properly to service important public needs like health, safety, environmental protection, or competition itself. And where government does intervene, it should choose the least restrictive means available, like taxes or disclosure, before turning to self-perpetuating "command and control" regulations.

This is the approach I took in eliminating the anticompetitive regulation of the airline industry. As a result of the Airline Deregulation Act of 1978—which one conservative economic group has heralded as the only deflationary legislation in the 95th Congress— consumers now fly at cheaper rates, and the industry makes greater profits than would otherwise have been possible in these times of spiraling fuel expenses. This is also the approach I have taken in reforming regulation of the trucking and drug industries.

This Congress, I have introduced comprehensive regulatory reform legislation, now pending before the Judiciary Committee, which establishes a mechanism to review our entire regulatory process on an agency-by-agency basis. Only by using this painstaking approach, can we successfully remove the "heavy hand" of government regulation from the marketplace and improve the ability of our agencies to promote the public interest.

In the last several years, there has been an increased concern with environmental protection. How would you achieve a balance between the need for economic growth and protection of the environment?

We have a responsibility to all Americans, whether they work in industrial plants, on farms, or in urban offices to protect our environmental situation. Among other things, 70 to 90 percent of cancer is environmentally caused, and we must remain committed to policies that will reduce that incidence. I think American industry has the resiliency to retool, in environmentally sound ways, with appropriate tax incentives. In addition, temporary federal subsidies such as that given to Chrysler are appropriate measures anticipating conversion of a significant portion of our industrial base to construction of mass transit, development of renewable energy sources such as solar and biomass fuel, and maximization of lowhead hydro.

I favor conversion of oil facilities to coal wherever that is possible to immediately reduce our disastrous dependency on foreign oil. Coal conversion can be achieved without harsh consequences for the environment. Beyond coal conversion, which would save a million barrels of oil a day, I have introduced legislation which through encouraging conservation and energy efficiency will save another 4 million barrels of oil a day by 1990—a greater saving than the administration's plan, at one-half the cost. It will provide an additional 731,000 jobs by 1990. Still another million barrels of oil a day can be saved through aggressive development of solar energy sources and responsible, converted synfuel development.

The survival of our free economy depends on making wise investment now which will return billions in wealth and save billions later that we would otherwise have to spend on health care. The problems we face require strong and careful management, not harsh solutions. There is no fundamental conflict between managing our resources wisely and enjoying a strong and healthy economy; it is quite the contrary.

What should the United States stand for in world affairs in the 1980s? Concretely how would you propose that American ideals and interests prevail?

America's situation internationally has lurched from crisis to crisis under the Carter administration. U.S. prestige has dropped around the world. Our allies have lost confidence in us and our adversaries have lost respect.

I believe the primary obligation of the president is to reassert our strength in a credible fashion, reassure our allies, and reclaim our standard as the defenders of freedom.

A strong defense is the cornerstone of foreign policy, and I support military spending and strengthened intelligence capabilities necessary to assure the national security of the United States. I am in favor of both effective, verifiable arms control agreements and critically important weapons systems like Trident, cruise missiles, a larger navy, and appropriate pay and compensation for military personnel.

With regard to the Soviet Union, I prefer predictable, firm, and credible policies that ensure unacceptable costs for aggression. But, let us not foreclose every opening to the Soviet Union. Afghanistan is not the first abuse of Soviet power, nor will it be the last, and it must not become the end of the world. Ten months after the Cuban

Missile Crisis—a far greater threat to American security than Afghanistan—the U.S. Senate ratified the nuclear test ban treaty by an overwhelming vote.

The task of statesmanship is to convince the Russians that there is a reason for fear, but also reason for hope, in their relations with the United States.

Throughout my seventeen years in public life, I have been a staunch supporter of Israel's freedom. Israel is a bulwark to our security, and it is a democratic ally in the Middle East.

I also believe the United States should expand cooperation with Mexico on the important issues of energy, immigration, and trade. I first called for a North American Energy Alliance with Mexico and Canada in 1971.

Finally, I have consistently and effectively supported human rights and political freedoms around the world. I have successfully sponsored legislation to cut off aid to military regimes such as Chile and Argentina, reunited large numbers of divided families from the Soviet Union, Eastern Europe, and China, and have persisted in my efforts to assist refugees around the world.

What would be the elements of your defense policy? How would you ensure the success of your vision of America's future in a changing and troubled world?

In building a strong national defense—the cornerstone of an effective foreign policy—I believe the essential element is the possession of usable force. Our four armed services, now more than ever, must be ready, reliable, and combat effective if we are to defend our national interests, whenever and wherever challenged.

A military lesson of the post–World War II era is that nuclear and gold-plated conventional weapons have tended to make us missile bound and less combat ready. That is why, as we look ahead at the decade before us, our emphasis should be not only on strategic deterrence but on developing and strengthening a general purpose force that is fighting-trim, equipped with workable and working weapons, and relevant and ready for the conduct of various regional missions.

The military balance between the United States and the Soviet Union is central in discussing national defense. Soviet military forces are now the equal of our own; approximate military parity is a fact of life. I have no doubts that in this decade the Soviet Union will steadily work to improve its military forces—upgrading the accuracy of its strategic forces, deploying a new generation of aircraft and armed vehicles, and strengthening its ability to reach foreign lands beyond Afghanistan and other nearby places.

Similarly, the United States must modernize and expand its military force in concert with its Atlantic and Pacific allies, in response to increased turbulence in such vital regions as the Middle East, the Persian Gulf, and southwest Asia, and in relation to the capabilities of the USSR. The crucial question is how do we accomplish the important task of strengthening our forces and making them usable, so that they are a credible deterrent and capable of defending Western interests.

One certain way *not* to improve America's capability is to engage in an empty debate over arbitrary percentages of budget growth. Anyone who is serious about national defense knows what the nation needs is not a 3 percent, 5 percent, or 7 percent solution in defense spending. National security cannot be purchased by merely spending more money. What we need are defense resources effectively directed to actual military requirements and assurances that our nation can rely upon capable and cost-effective military weapons. I have in mind such weapons as the air-launched cruise missile, which provides us with a military advantage at far less than what it costs the Soviet Union to counter it. I have in mind that these weapons be manned by skilled and experienced personnel. And I have in mind that our armed forces be headed by committed and confident leadership. Those are the criteria that I believe will guarantee a strong defense and those are the criteria I shall apply when analyzing and voting on the fiscal 1981 defense budget.

In recent years presidents of both parties have had great difficulty in getting Congress to adopt the programs they have recommended. What has caused this difficulty, and how would you go about overcoming it?

There are a number of reasons for the past discord between the executive and legislative branches. During previous administrations, there was a tendency to disregard congressional concerns and interests until after all decisions had been made by the White House. During the Nixon years, this factor dominated the congressional atmosphere. The programs then being offered tended in the eyes of a majority of the Congress to be contrary to the best interests of the country and ignorant of congressional responsibilities—even constitutional obligations. To a degree, the current administration has also failed to keep Congress informed during the preparation of its major legislative proposals. Second, the Congress itself has undergone internal changes in which traditional mechanisms for maintaining internal party discipline have been undermined. Third, during the current administration the effort to build a coalition for a particular legislative proposal has all too often begun far too late. Finally, this administration has ignored the responsibility of the president to present to the country a forceful explanation of his programs which can contribute to an atmosphere which then helps encourage congressional cooperation.

During my years in the Congress, I have worked closely on many issues with senators from both parties and from all over the nation. Many of my legislative proposals which have been adopted, including the forty health bills of mine which have been enacted, have brought together members of both parties and members from different regions and ideological backgrounds. As president I believe I can achieve a national partnership for many of my legislative proposals by building public support for my initiatives from the outset, by bringing congressional involvement early in the development of legislation, by recognizing the real and different concerns of individual members of Congress and senators and dealing with them frankly, and by personally fighting to make them a reality.

What policies or programs will you pursue that best reflect your sense of domestic priorities for the 1980s and beyond? What sacrifices will the American people be asked to make?

The strongest social program America can have is a sound economy. The irretrievable mismanagement of the economy by this administration necessitates imposition of a six-month wage-price freeze, followed by mandatory controls, coupled with gasoline rationing. These short-term measures must be coupled with immediate long-term steps to revive our economy and reduce our dependence on foreign energy sources. All of these actions will require sacrifices from the American people. For example, they will have to use less energy, especially gasoline, and the long-term measures to revitalize the economy will necessitate a higher rate of saving.

I am confident that, with these measures, we can get our economy moving again and when we are done, we will have more resources to assure a stable and bright future for ourselves and our children. Moreover, from that path of growth, I think we can obtain the funds necessary to pursue the priorities I believe are important: to rebuild and revitalize our cities, make health care available and affordable for all Americans, provide jobs for those for whom there are none available, improve educational opportunities, reform our welfare system, and pursue justice for minorities, women, the handicapped and others who still suffer from the gap between the American dream we all share and the hard realities that still persist.

Reagan

RONALD REAGAN was elected governor of California in 1966 and reelected in 1970. After completing his second term, he initiated a nationally syndicated radio commentary program and newspaper column. From 1974 to 1975 he was a member of the Presidential Commission investigating the CIA. He also served on the Board of Directors of the Committee on the Present Danger and founded Citizens for the Republic, a political action organization.

He graduated from Eureka College in 1932 with a degree in economics and sociology. After a brief career as a sports broadcaster and editor, he became an actor in films and television, serving six terms as president of the Screen Actors Guild and two terms as president of the Motion Picture Industry Council. During World War II, he served three years in the U.S. Army Air Corps. He was born in 1911, in Tampico, Ill.

How would you solve our nation's energy problems? Specifically, what would be the key elements of your national energy policy?

Looking at the fiasco we now call "the energy crisis," there is not one straight answer, nor any realistic hope of relief, to come from the present administration in three years of federal treatment of the problem.

Currently, U.S. policies are geared toward decreasing demand, regulating markets, and lowering growth. We see the results of these policies in price controls, plans for rationing, energy taxes, withdrawals of lands from mining and petroleum exploration, thoughts of banning weekend driving, and a foreign policy increasingly dictated by foreign producers. To pay for these constraints and restrictions, we face more taxes and big budgets to feed the regulatory machinery—which leads, inexorably, to more inflation.

We need more energy, and that means diversifying our sources of supply away from the OPEC countries. It means more efficient automobiles. It also means more exploration and development of oil and natural gas here in our own country. The only way to free ourselves from the power of OPEC is to be less dependent on outside sources of fuel.

The answer is more domestic production of oil and gas. We need wider use of nuclear power within strict safety rules. We need more research and development by energy industries in substitutes for fossil fuels. We need an overhaul of antiquated depreciation tax codes. We need a capital market that can draw on real savings. We need an equity market with confidence in this nation's real commitment to growth.

In years to come solar energy may provide an answer, but for the next two or three decades we need to do such things as master the chemistry of coal. Putting the market system to work for these objectives is an essential first step for their achievement.

Most polls show that Americans consider inflation to be the number one domestic problem. How would you rid the economy of inflation?

I'll attack inflation sensibly.

First, I will tell our monetary authorities that they have only one job—to restore and maintain a sound dollar at home and abroad. Deficits may tempt the government to print new dollars, instead of paying back its debt with honest money. We must remove that temptation by balancing the budget, but we do not have to succumb to it in the meantime.

Second, I will ask Congress to act immediately in beginning the necessary reform of our tax system. In 1979 personal income increased 12 percent, but taxes rose at a faster rate, up 15.8 percent. Mr. Carter's new budget projects total tax receipts to be 21.6 percent of GNP in 1981 and 24.2 percent of GNP in 1985, *an all-time historic high for peacetime or wartime.*

We need to restore the rewards for working and saving by cutting income tax rates and adjusting them automatically for inflation. My goal will be to cut the tax rates of all Americans by approximately 30 percent during my first term in office.

Third, I will attack excessive federal spending. The U.S. General Accounting Office says that up to $50 billion, or one-tenth of the federal budget, is simply wasted every year.

Finally, I believe we need to accept the fact that federal over-regulation of the economy has exceeded the bounds of sensibility. Where costs exceed benefits, the regulators must desist.

Inflation is not caused by people or businesses. And you don't cure inflation by removing the nation's incentive to grow strong once again.

The productivity growth rate of the American economy declined drastically in the 1970s. During 1979 it was negative. What steps would you take to restore productivity growth to the American economy? Do you believe we need to stimulate capital formation to aid in this? How would you do this?

We're right in worrying about declining American productivity. Higher productivity means we can produce more with the same effort. It takes people who have better ideas. It takes people with savings to invest in those ideas. And it takes motivated workers to implement them.

You can't increase productivity by making people at every level work harder for less pay. They need better tools and rewards equal to their effort.

By blaming Americans themselves for being less productive, the government is again ignoring the effect of its own policies. The federal income tax is a tax on all individual productivity—on labor, on savings and investment, on enterprise. These tax rates climb steeply with income. But what's worse, they are not adjusted for inflation. Every time inflation raises your income, but not your buying power, you are still pushed into a higher tax bracket. Over the past decade, this combination of inflation and steep tax rates has reduced the rewards for higher productivity, and individual productivity has suffered.

When government takes more of one person's income the larger it is, and gives it to someone else for having a smaller income, each person suddenly has more to lose by earning more. The government has effectively raised the tax on the effort of both.

Americans have not become too lazy to work, or complacent with their accomplishments. We are being punished for working, for saving, for investing, for growing, by a thoughtless government which is quickly becoming the major partner in their families' income.

Government regulation provides benefits, but it also imposes costs. What changes in the regulatory process, if any, would you propose?

We need to reexamine our entire approach to federal regulation. Regulations are a form of tax. It's now well documented that complying with mushrooming government regulation adds over $120 billion to the cost of doing business, and therefore to the cost of living, every single year.

Those regulations which limit someone's wages, prices, interest, or other income don't reduce inflation. They reduce our productivity and economic efficiency, and worsen inflation. We need to abolish such controls.

We also need to change regulations which penalize the young

or the old, such as the earnings limit on the retired and their survivors, and the high minimum wage required before teenagers may be given a job. Every federal agency needs to be required to weigh both costs and benefits before imposing new regulations.

And all agencies need to be subject to a single "regulatory budget" which limits the overall yearly cost to the nation of complying with federal regulations.

In the last several years, there has been an increased concern with environmental protection. How would you achieve a balance between the need for economic growth and protection of the environment?

I think our heightened concern for the environment is probably one of the most positive outgrowths of the 1960s.

During that decade, we were shocked into the realization that we were harming the environment, in many cases irreparably.

As governor of California during the last half of that decade, and the first half of the 1970s, I was proud to have helped increase both public awareness of environmental problems and to have initiated both workable and lasting protection measures.

At the federal level, however, government may have lost its sense of balance in this area. While we need not blindly seek growth at terrible cost to the environment, neither should we so excessively pursue "environmentalism" that we endanger the economic health and expanded job opportunities which are essential to the future of our people.

To achieve a sound environmental policy—a balance between economic growth and ecological protection—we need to reexamine each regulatory requirement with a commitment to simplify and to streamline the process.

Moreover, we need to return to the states the primary responsibility for environmental regulation and thus increase responsiveness to local conditions.

This is how we strike, more accurately, the delicate balance between protecting this land and promoting its people's economic progress.

What should the United States stand for in world affairs in the 1980s? Concretely how would you propose that American ideals and interests prevail?

In my view, the United States must first decide upon its priorities for the 1980s and then move swiftly to formulate and implement realistic policies to achieve those priorities. Central to this task must be a long-range strategy designed to protect American interests and create conditions of stability in our economy and in the world in which global economic order can expand.

If a single word could be used to describe the 1970s, "disappointment" might be an appropriate one. Not only did we fall short of achieving a durable peace based on solid accomplishments, but we actually retreated from the world, often as though we should be ashamed of ourselves for past misdeeds.

I do not think that we can enter the decade of the 1980s with an outlook of gloom or despair; rather, the "image" we present to the world must faithfully reflect the reality of America, its values and its goals.

Because so many of the world look up to our country as a living example of freedom in action, and while I believe we must live up to those expectations whenever possible, the challenge of the 1980s demands that we once again pursue our national interest with the resources at our disposal. Without behaving in a narrow, nationalistic way, we must put American interests first.

This means rebuilding our dissipated strength, and the best way—indeed the only way—to do this is by releasing the vitality of our great country from the artificial restraints of massive governmental regulation which we ourselves have imposed on it. Remove those restraints, restore individual initiative, and provide the conditions for rapid, dynamic growth in all sectors of our lives: those are the essential preconditions for pursuing an active role in the world and for defending our vital interests.

What would be the elements of your defense policy? How would you ensure the success of your vision of America's future in a changing and troubled world?

My first priority would be to embark on a program of rebuilding American military strength. Selectively and prudently, we must commit our resources to achieving this goal.

We have permitted ourselves the luxury of believing that our principal adversary, the Soviet Union, shares our hopes for peace and our trust in mutual restraint through good example. That this leads to policies endangering our national security is now abundantly clear.

At a minimum, we must move quickly to restore the principal elements of the last Republican defense budget and just as swiftly establish strategic goals.

Finding the resources to do this job will definitely not be easy, but I believe we can take an initial step by redirecting the misspent resources presently being consumed by a huge governmental bureaucracy. This cannot be done effectively, or at all, without the assistance of the Congress.

Specifically, restoring the credibility of our deterrent power must come before anything can be accomplished.

In recent years presidents of both parties have had great difficulty in getting Congress to adopt the programs they have recommended. What has caused this difficulty, and how would you go about overcoming it?

Congress has, indeed, become increasingly independent, reflecting perhaps a national mood of suspicion of those in authority. We need to remember that Congress was severely—and unfairly—criticized during Watergate for having abandoned its responsibility.

Members of the House, insisting on greater autonomy, have curbed the seniority system and created literally dozens of new subcommittees. As one would expect, this led to today's diffusion of power. Many newer congressmen are given unprecedented authority. One result is the diminution of House leaders' traditional power.

Vastly increased media coverage and better communications brought the Senate into national focus and made ombudsmen of individual senators. And the increase over the past two decades in "presidential senators" is testament to a new spirit of upward mobility and national aspirations within the Senate itself.

Gaining acceptance and passage of any president's program, therefore, depends on the program being right in the first place, perceived by both Congress and the nation as such, and evolved in closer cooperation with Congress and its leaders than is the case today.

What policies or programs will you pursue that best reflect your sense of domestic priorities for the 1980s and beyond? What sacrifices will the American people be asked to make?

Someone once said that the difference between an American and any other kind of person is that an American lives in anticipation of the future because he knows it will be a great place. Other people fear the future as just a repetition of past failures. There's a lot of truth in that. If there is one thing we are sure of it is that history need not be relived, that nothing is impossible, and that man is capable of improving his circumstances beyond what we are told is fact.

The crisis we face is not the result of any failure of the American spirit; it is a failure of our leaders to establish rational goals and give our people something to order their lives by.

71

No problem we face today can compare with the need to restore the health of the American economy and the strength of the American dollar. The people have not created this disaster in our economy; the federal government has. It has overspent, overestimated, and overregulated.

We need to put an end to the arrogance of a federal establishment which accepts no blame for our condition, cannot be relied upon to give us a fair estimate of our situation, and utterly refuses to live within its means. We need to review the functions of the federal government to determine which of those are the proper province of levels of government closer to the people. Finally, we need to force the entire federal bureaucracy to live in the real world of reduced spending, streamlined functions, and accountability to the people it serves.